MAKE YOUR OWN
DINOSAURS

MAKE YOUR OWN
DINOSAURS

ANAYA PUBLISHERS LTD
LONDON

First published in Great Britain in 1994
by Anaya Publishers Ltd, Strode House,
44-50 Osnaburgh Street, London NW1 3ND

Editor   Emma Callery
Design   Watermark Communications Group Ltd
Photographer   Shona Wood
Illustrator   Stephen Dew

British Library in Cataloguing Data

Dean, Audrey Vincente
   Make Your Own Dinosaurs
   I. Title
   745. 592

ISBN 1-85470-177-0

Typeset in Great Britain by Litho Link Ltd, Welshpool, Powys
Colour reproduction by Scantrans Pte Ltd, Singapore
Printed and bound in Hong Kong

Contents

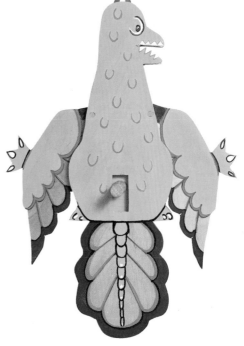

Introduction

Dinosaurs can be made from all sorts of things ranging from felt and fabric to salt dough, wood and even black plastic bags. Here is a varied collection of extraordinary dinosaurs, all of which are easy to make.

Dinosaurs have always fascinated adults and children alike. To this day there exists an aura of mystery about these startling creatures. No one yet knows how they came to exist, or why they became extinct. The details of their lives and habits are still the subject of painstaking work by scientists.

Dinosaurs have replaced dragons and mythical beasts which have always appeared in folk lore and literature. As fresh discoveries are still reported from time to time, dinosaurs form a link between mythology and our continuing interest in the world about us.

The word "dinosaur" comes from two Greek words meaning "terrible lizard". It was a word which first came into existence in 1841, invented by Professor Richard Owen, one of the first scientists who began serious work on their study.

As early as 1853, dinosaurs began to catch the imagination in the way they do today. In that year the inventor of the new word gave a banquet in honour of 20 eminent guests, who were seated, with some difficulty, inside a replica of a largely imaginary Iguanodon. At the seven course dinner the Professor himself, as host, sat inside the head of the dinosaur at the top of the table. The invitations sent to the lucky guests showed the scene of the banquet in the background, while a reclining Pterodactyl in the foreground extended his wing on which details of the invitation were written.

From that moment until the present day the subject has provided rich opportunities for the imagination, from stories such as *The Lost World* by Sir Arthur Conan Doyle, to Stephen Spielberg's terrifying film, *Jurassic*

Park. Such adventures become all the more exciting as more and more knowledge comes to light.

Dinosaurs continue to fascinate with their strange names, their size and their varied and fantastic shapes. Even the fact that nothing is known of the colours of their outward appearance gives scope to the imagination, for it means that a picture or model of a dinosaur can be coloured however you like.

What could be more stimulating for a book of varied craft work based on these wonderful creatures?

I have tried to devise projects which will encourage further interest. Since a good picture of the dinosaur you are making is needed, one of the many illustrated books available is sure to give you ideas for other models. The instructions for the papier-mâché Tyrannosaurus rex or the salt dough Diplodocus could be easily adapted to make other dinosaurs.

Many of the designs can be made by children without help, such as the Brachiosaurus puppet or the "Dinattack" board game. Some will need a little assistance from adults, depending on the age of the child.

Others involve different crafts: papier-mâché makes the dino baby's egg while simple knitting makes the body; the lampshade and book cover are stencilled, the T-shirt is decorated with fabric crayons, and the jeans are appliquéd. Simple woodwork, in the Archaeopteryx coat hanger or Triceratops box is included. There are many opportunities in the designs for exciting colouring and painting.

I have also tried to use scrap or inexpensive materials, so that they can be tried out in the spirit of fun. If, for instance, you would like to make the Battling Pachycephalosaurs and your first effort is not quite right, it will cost you nothing to save another empty cereal box and try again. I used three before my model would work well.

I wish you all a happy time. Except for one or two designs which are pure flights of fancy, all the dinosaurs really existed, and at the end of the book I have given an alphabetical list of them, with a very short description.

ONE

Model dinosaurs

❧

Battling Pachycephalosaurs

Adapt this idea to make your own fighting dinosaurs! Make the model from scrap materials and paint it with bright colours.

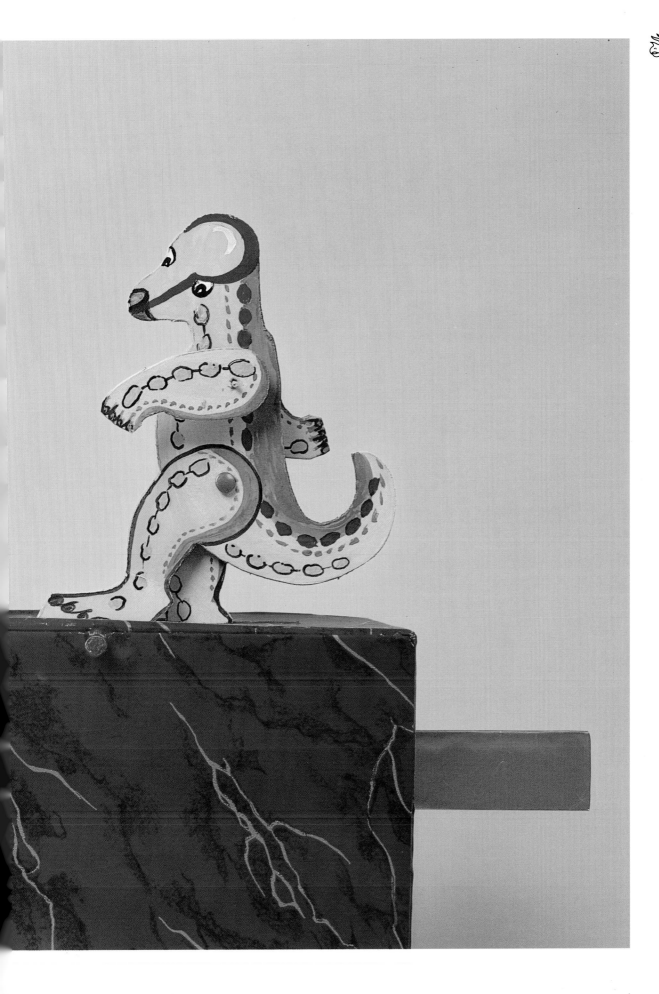

Materials

5 × 15in (13 × 38cm) of thick card
Paper for patterns
1 empty cardboard cereal box
Sheet of gift wrap paper
Adhesive for paper or spray glue
4 paper fasteners with pronged ends
4 copper coins, each approx 1in (2.5cm)
    diameter
Short length of masking tape
Approx 8in (20cm) of ¼in (6mm) dowel or
    a medium thickness plastic knitting
    needle
2 cocktail or match sticks
4 approx ⅛in (4mm) beads with large holes

Preparation

1 Cut a strip of card to work the model,
1in (2.5cm) wide by the length of the box
plus 6in (15cm). Mark centre of the card
strip and points for holes 3in (7.5cm) on
either side of the centre.

2 Trace patterns for the dinosaur bodies,
opposite, including all the points for holes
and other details. Transfer the outlines and
details to the remainder of the thick card
and cut 1 complete body, 1 back leg and 2
arms for each figure.

Working the design

3 Cover the box with gift wrap paper.
Make sure it is well stuck down. If you are
using cold water paste and your box is
smooth and glossy you will need to scratch
the surface well with the tip of a craft knife
to make the paper adhere.

4 To make the dinosaur platform, rule one
of the long sides of the box with guide lines
1-5 as shown overleaf. Lightly rule line 1
across the centre from front to back. Lines
2 and 3 are each 1½in (4cm) on either side
of line 1. Line 4 is ¾in (2cm) away from the
back edge of the box, and line 5 is ½in
(12mm) in front of line 4. Mark positions
of slots A and B for the back legs and slots
C and D for the front legs. Using a sharp
craft knife carefully cut the slots ⅛in
(3mm) wide, through all layers of paper and

card. The slots must be cut within lines 2
and 3. Their inner edges must be straight,
to ensure smooth working of the model.

5 For the working strip, cut ⅛in (3mm)
wide slots in both ends of the box,
positioned as shown overleaf.

6 For the front leg pivots, make holes in
the back and front of the box at either end
of lines 2 and 3, ½in (12mm) below the top
of the box. Enlarge the holes to fit the
dowel or knitting needle, which will make
the pivots.

7 You will need to reach the interior of the
box to assemble the working parts. At the
back of the box, cut a trapdoor 4in (10cm)
deep within 1¼in (3cm) of the two side
edges and top. Bend the trapdoor outwards
and downwards. It can be fastened back in
place later.

8 To make the Pachycephalosaurs, make
small holes by rotating the points of the
scissors at each marked position E, F, G and
H. Some of them will need to be enlarged
later. Paint or colour one surface of each
piece to make a pair of figures.

Pieces for the Pachycephalosaurus' bodies.
Trace off actual size

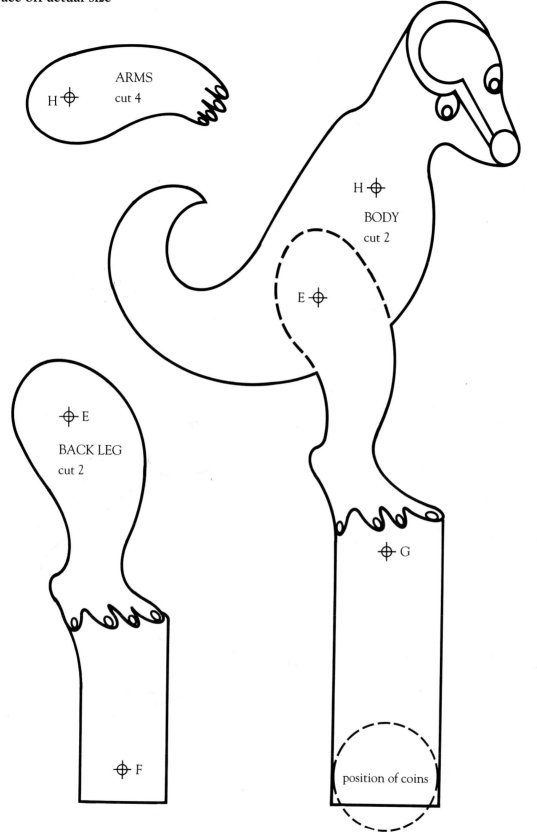

ARMS
cut 4

H

H

BODY
cut 2

E

E

BACK LEG
cut 2

G

F

position of coins

9 Enlarge holes marked E in the back legs to fit paper fasteners loosely. Place the back legs behind the bodies and push the fasteners through from front to back, then open the prongs to secure them. Make sure the legs will move easily.

10 For the front legs, enlarge holes G so that they fit the pivot loosely. Push the front legs through slots A and B and the back legs through slots C and D. Use a wrapping of masking tape to fasten a coin to either side of each card below the front legs, as indicated by the dotted line in the diagram showing the body pieces. Cut 2 lengths from the dowel or knitting needle each the width of the top plus 1in (2.5cm) and push them through the box and holes G in the front legs. Stick ends in place.

11 For the back legs, insert the working strip through the box from side to side, in front of the weighted ends of the front legs. Insert a paper fastener through holes F in the back legs, and through corresponding holes in the working strip.

12 Next, attach the arms to the bodies using the cocktail or match sticks and beads. If necessary, pare them with a craft knife to fit the holes in the beads. Enlarge holes H in the bodies to fit the sticks loosely. Push each stick through an arm from front to back, through a bead, the body, another bead and lastly the front of the other arm. Adjust the arms so that one is up and the other down. Cut the sticks close to the arms and secure the ends with a drop of glue. The arms should pivot loosely.

Finishing
13 Close the trap door at the back of the box and stick a piece of gift wrap over the cut.

14 To make the Pachycephalosaurs fight push the working strip up and down, from side to side, or gently move it in a see saw action.

Positions of guidelines and slots.

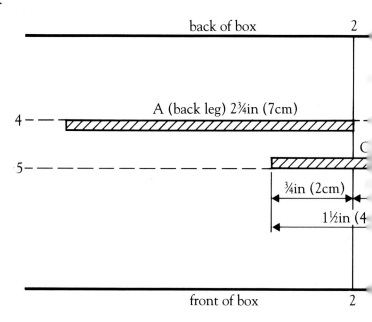

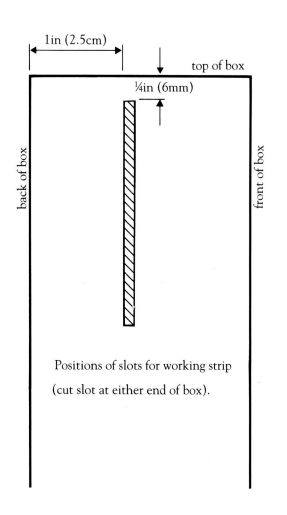

Positions of slots for working strip

(cut slot at either end of box).

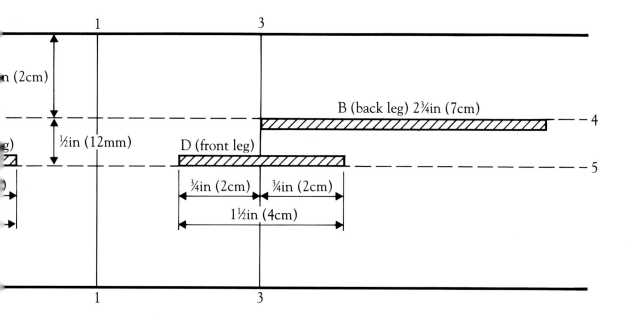

n (2cm)

½in (12mm)

B (back leg) 2¾in (7cm) — 4

D (front leg) — 5

¾in (2cm) ¾in (2cm)

1½in (4cm)

The back view showing inside workings

15

Salt dough Diplodocus

Models of chunky dinosaurs are easy to make in salt dough. Diplodocus was the longest dinosaur of them all: about as long as a tennis court.

Materials
1 mug salt
4 mugs plain flour
Approximately 1½ mugs water
White or light colour emulsion paint
Paints
Silver marker
Matt varnish

Preparation
1 The amounts of the ingredients are given by volume, not by weight. If you need more salt dough, multiply the quantities by volume. Put the salt and flour into a large bowl and gradually mix in the water with a knife and a wooden spoon. Stop adding water when the dough clings together well, neither too sticky nor too dry. Remove the dough and knead it by hand until it is smooth and pliable. It should hold any modelled shape well. Prepared dough will keep for several weeks in a refrigerator if it is well wrapped in plastic.

The seven body parts.

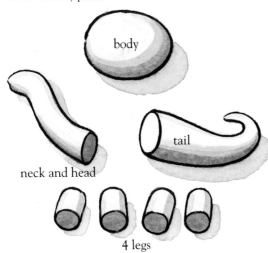

body

neck and head

tail

4 legs

Making the Diplodocus
2 A good picture of a Diplodocus is a great help. This model is made in 7 pieces which are body, neck, tail and 4 legs. You can practise making it using the same dough as many times as you like.

3 Although the proportions may be varied, roughly divide the dough into quarters. Model one piece into an egg shape for the body. With the palm of your hand roll

another quarter into a sausage shape for the neck, making it a little thinner and more rounded at one end for the head and quite flat across the other end so that it can be joined to the body. Roll another quarter of the dough into a tapering sausage for the long tail, keeping one end quite flat, again, for ease of joining. Divide the remaining quarter into 5 and roll 4 of them into short fat sausages for the legs. Keep the last piece of dough to join the various parts together later.

4 To harden the dough, lay the pieces on a baking tray and put them in a low oven, 175°F (80°C/gas mark ¼). They will take approximately 1½-2 hours. To check if they are cooked right through, tap them with a fork. Dough which is not cooked right through will sound duller than the pinging noise made by a thoroughly hardened piece (see Better Techniques).

5 Using a paint brush, moisten the places to be joined with water and use the surplus piece of dough to make joints. Press a little on the moistened part and push the adjacent part into the fresh dough. Neaten the joint by scraping off the surplus dough and smoothing it with water. The various parts will have been flattened where they were placed on the baking sheet to harden. This can be corrected by applying water and more dough. Leave the model to dry as before in a low oven.

Finishing
6 Paint the model, first giving it a base coat of emulsion paint. Finally give it a light coat of matt varnish.

Centrosaurus soft toy

This is a dinosaur to hug. Make him in brilliant colours. He belongs to a family of dinosaurs called Ceratopians, which used their horns and neck frills mainly for fighting.

Materials

Paper for patterns
20in (50cm) of 45in (115cm) fabric in
    main colour
12in (30cm) of 45in (115cm) fabric in
    contrast
12in (30cm) square felt in contrast
Scraps of black and white felt
Embroidery cotton to match contrast felt
Two 2lb (1kg) bags of toy stuffing
Sewing cottons
Two 6in (15cm) pipe cleaners

Preparation

1 This toy is 17in (43cm) long by 10in (25cm) tall. Draw the pattern pieces on squared paper from the graph patterns on pages 21-23. Put in all marks, letters and words. Seam allowances of ¼in (6mm) have been given. From main colour fabric cut 2 side bodies including tail, 1 head gusset, 4 outer legs, 4 paw pads and 2 half neck frills. Do not cut out darts on outer legs.

2 From contrast fabric cut 2 of underbody reversing patterns to give a pair; 1 of undertail, 4 inner legs, 2 half neck frills.

3 From contrast felt cut 2 horns, 4 sets of claws and 18 frill spikes. From black felt cut 2 eye backings and 2 pupils. From white felt cut 2 eyes.

Making the Centrosaurus

4 For the body and tail, with right sides facing, stitch from A under the snout to B. Leave B-C open for head gusset and stitch from C to D to E under the tail. Join in the head gusset matching B and C on either side. On the underbody, with right sides facing, join F-G leaving about 4in (10cm) open in centre of seam for stuffing.

5 Join H-G-H on underbody to H-G-H on undertail. Press seams open. With right sides facing, pin and baste underbody and undertail to body, starting at A on the body and ending at E under the tail. Turn to right side and stuff body and tail very firmly. Stitch underbody opening.

6 For the legs, close darts on outer legs. With right sides facing, join side seams of outer to inner legs. Pin and baste seam allowance to wrong side at top and bottom of legs. Pin and baste a claw set round the bottom of each leg, positioning each so that the fold of the seam touches the dotted line on the claw set.

7 Baste the seam allowance of the leg bases to the wrong side and hand sew them in position to the bottoms of the legs. Stuff the legs very firmly. Pin them to the body as shown in the photograph on the previous page, making sure the dinosaur can stand firmly and oversew in place by hand using double thread.

8 For the neck frill, close darts on main colour and contrast pieces of the neck frill. With right sides facing, join seams I-J on both pairs. Snip into seam allowances and press seam open. With right sides facing, join assembled main colour frill to contrast frill, leaving space to turn. Insert the pipe cleaners between the layers of fabric and catch in place along the seam of the main colour part. Close opening.

9 Oversew frill spikes together in pairs putting a little stuffing between each pair before the sewing is complete. Catch them to outer edge of the contrast side of the neck frill spacing them evenly.

Finishing

10 Sew the neck frill to the head so that the centre of the straight edge is 2¾in (7cm) behind the front point of the head gusset. Oversew the edges of the horn together, leaving the straight base open. Stuff firmly and sew to head over the front end of the head gusset. Catch the white felt eyes over the eye bases and sew the black centres on top, embroidering 2 straight stitches in the middle of the black in white for highlights. Embroider the mouth in a double line of stem stitch using 6 strands of embroidery cotton.

The body pieces.

1 square = 2in (5cm)

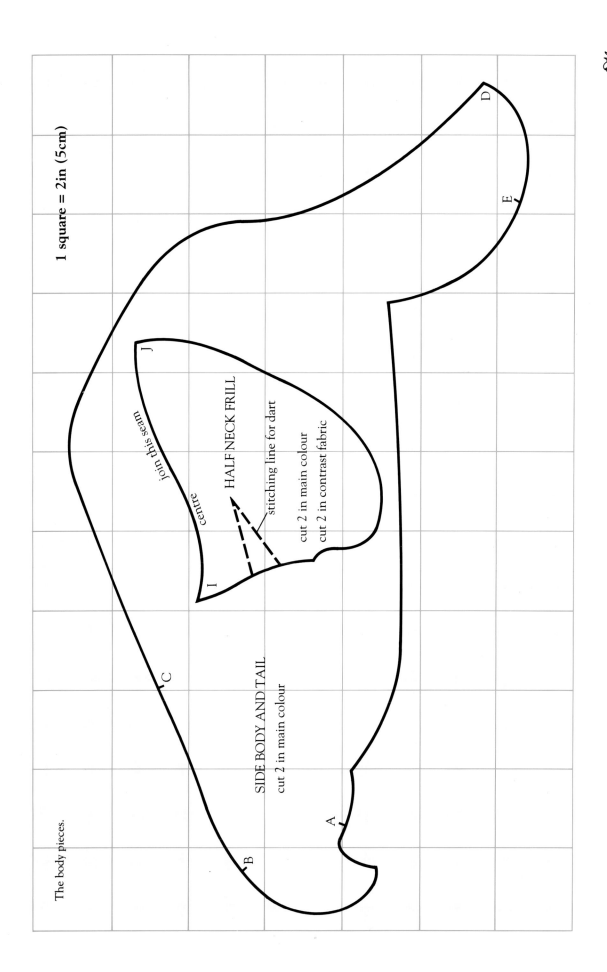

join this seam

centre

I

J

HALF NECK FRILL

stitching line for dart

cut 2 in main colour
cut 2 in contrast fabric

SIDE BODY AND TAIL

cut 2 in main colour

A

B

C

D

E

MODEL DINOSAURS

1 square = 2in (5cm)

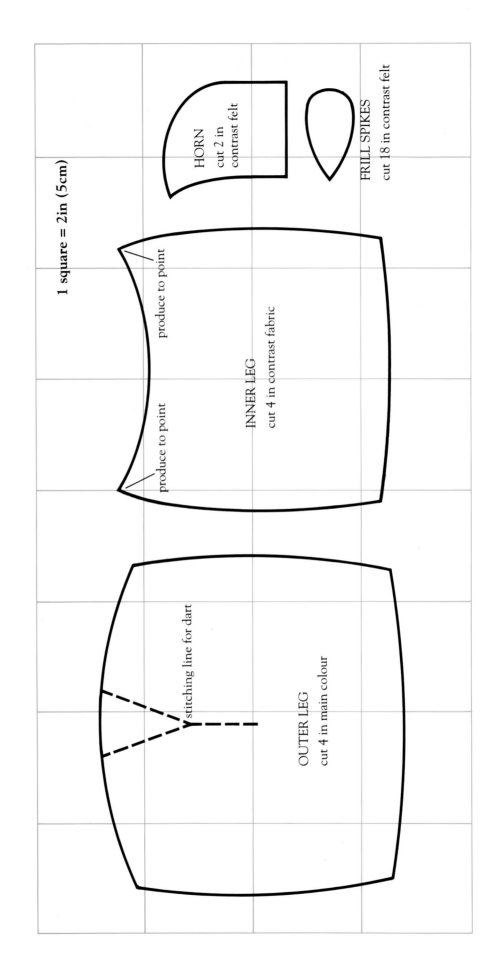

HORN
cut 2 in
contrast felt

FRILL SPIKES
cut 18 in contrast felt

produce to point

produce to point

INNER LEG
cut 4 in contrast fabric

produce to point

stitching line for dart

OUTER LEG
cut 4 in main colour

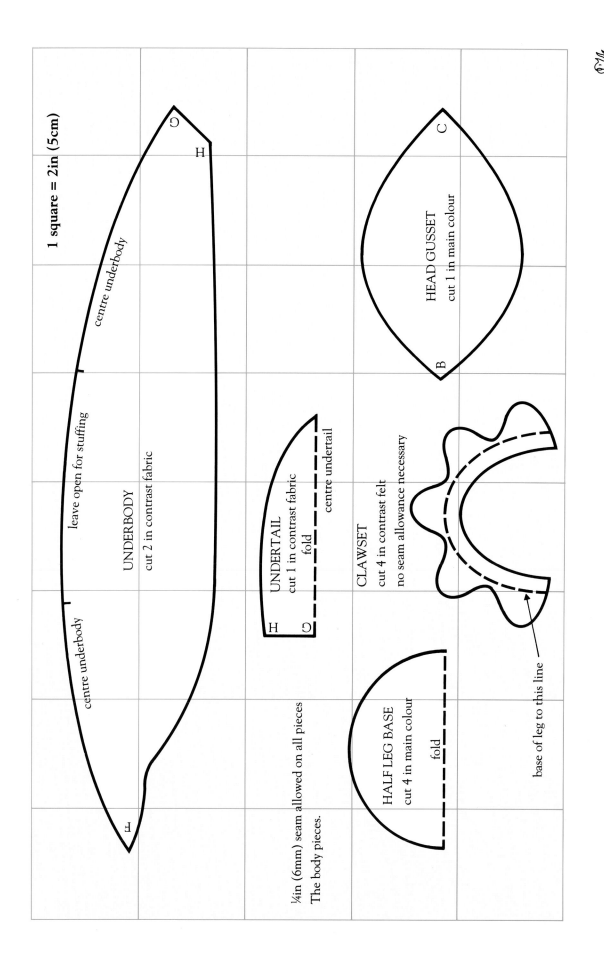

1 square = 2in (5cm)

centre underbody

leave open for stuffing

centre underbody

UNDERBODY
cut 2 in contrast fabric

G

H

F

UNDERTAIL
cut 1 in contrast fabric
fold

centre undertail

H   G

CLAWSET
cut 4 in contrast felt
no seam allowance necessary

base of leg to this line

HALF LEG BASE
cut 4 in main colour
fold

HEAD GUSSET
cut 1 in main colour

C

B

¼in (6mm) seam allowed on all pieces
The body pieces.

Corythosaurus family

Soft sculpture using felt and scraps of material makes this jolly family of Corythosaurus, complete with pet Dimetro-Doggy.

Materials

Paper for patterns

Two 9in (23cm) squares of felt for grandad, in different shades

6in (15cm) squares of felt for rest of family, 2 shades will be needed for each dinosaur

Scraps of felt in 2 or 3 shades of green for Dimetro-Doggy

Polyester stuffing

Assorted beads, scraps of ribbon and sequins

Scraps of embroidery thread

2-4 pipe cleaners for each dinosaur

Preparation

1 Trace the pattern pieces overleaf. The pattern given will make the grandad, 8in (20cm) high. For the father, reduce the redrawn pattern photographically by 12%, for the mother reduce it by 30%, for the children reduce it by 50%. Cut pieces as given on patterns. No seam allowance is needed. Using small stitches, mark points E and F on side bodies and on contrast leg and arm pieces.

Making the Corythosaurs

2 All the dinosaurs are made in the same way. Oversew close to the edge on the wrong sides. Close darts in side bodies. Place side bodies together, wrong sides facing, matching darts. Oversew all round from A to the tip of the tail and along the back to D on the snout. Leaving D-C open,

sew from C to B. Insert the gusset and join one side of the body only from B to A. Turn to right side. Stuff body firmly through openings. Close gusset opening. Fold C-D flat so that central seams match and oversew, gathering slightly.

3 For each pair of eyes take a tiny back stitch with doubled sewing cotton in the side of the head, then thread a small bead and a round white sequin. Push the needle through the head. Thread another sequin and bead for the other eye and finish off with a secure back stitch under the second sequin. If preferred, a circle of white felt and a french knot in embroidery cotton can be used for each eye.

4 Embroider the mouth in stem stitch and add a french knot for each nostril. For the crest, fold a 1½in (4cm) square of felt in half, curving the short ends and sew to centre of head as illustrated right.

5 To make the legs and arms, place main and contrast legs together and oversew, leaving straight base open. Reverse pieces for second leg to give a pair. On smaller dinosaurs you will need to leave a little of the leg seam open. Turn to right side. Fold a pipe cleaner in half and insert into leg, stuff leg firmly round pipe cleaner, then snip off excess. Close openings. Complete the arms in the same way, leaving a little of the seam open to turn work.

6 To joint arms and legs, insert approximately 12in (30cm) of buttonhole thread into a darning needle and double it. Take a tiny back stitch through point E as marked on the inner arm and leave a short length of thread hanging. Then push the needle right through the body at the corresponding point. Take another tiny back stitch in the other arm and insert the needle through the body again to emerge in the same place where you started. Pull the thread to make the arms firm, then tie in a secure knot and cut off the excess. Joint the legs in the same way.

Side head of dinosaur.

7 To make Dimetro-Doggy, place the 2 side bodies together and join from A round the tip of the snout to B; leave B-C open and join from C to D. Match A on the underbody to A on the side bodies and join the underbody in place to D and back to A. Turn to right side and stuff firmly. Cut a back frill ¾ × 2½in (18mm × 6cm) and snip one long edge into small scallops, gather the other edge and sew it into the back, closing the opening. Embroider french knots on the body and add features.

Finishing
8 Grandad has a woolly beard made from polyester stuffing and a twig walking stick. For father, cut a waistcoat 2½ × 7in (6 × 18cm), fold over one long edge for lapels and cut arm holes. Overlap at centre front and add 2 small beads for buttons. For mother, cut felt 2 × 4in (5 × 10cm) and roll up for the baby, cut one short end in a curve and oversew for snout, add crest and features. Dress the baby in a scrap of fabric for a shawl and sew him into his mother's arms. For the little girl, gather a piece of ribbon for the skirt and sew round her body. Add a bead necklace. For the little boy, sew a strip of fabric round the top of each leg and another strip in the same colour round the body. You may find it easier to do this before you joint the legs to the body. For Dimetro-Doggy, add a collar and lead.

25

Grandad body pieces.
trace off actual size

no seam allowance needed

D

C — leave open

ARM

✗ E

cut 2 in main colour

cut 2 in contrast colour

SIDE BODY

cut 2 in main colour

B

✗ E

insert gusset

✗ F

A

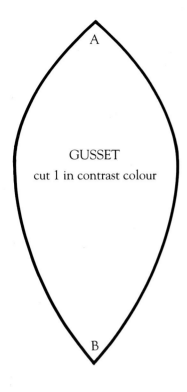

GUSSET
cut 1 in contrast colour

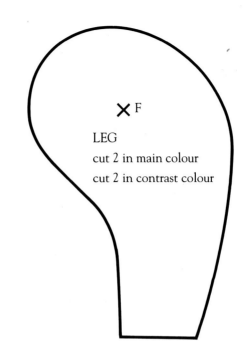

✗ F

LEG
cut 2 in main colour
cut 2 in contrast colour

Dimetro-Doggy body pieces.

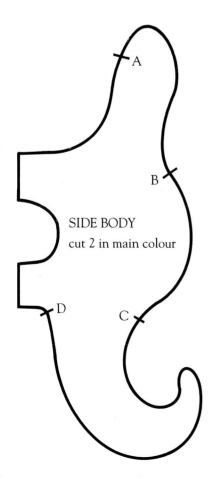

SIDE BODY
cut 2 in main colour

UNDERBODY

cut 1 in contrast colour

Tyrannosaurus rex

Using cardboard tubes and papier-mâché, this is a simple way of making a model. Paint it any colour you like: no one knows what colour dinosaurs were when they lived.

Materials
2 cardboard inner tubes from paper towel
    rolls, each about 9in (23cm) long
Sticky tape
Newspaper
5 hair rollers, each with 1½in (4cm)
    diameter made from wire coils with net
    covering
2 rollers ½in (12mm) diameter
Strong thread
Thin card
Wallpaper paste
Paper towels
Emulsion paint
Craft or poster paints
Small beads or buttons for eyes
Coloured foil

Preparation
1 Use the photograph of the Tyrannosaurus rex opposite to help you with its shape. Keep it in front of you as you work.

2 Push 1 of the paper towel tubes inside the other for about 1in (2.5cm) so that you have a tube about 16½in (41cm) long. Fasten the joint with sticky tape. Roll 3 double sheets of newspaper sideways and push them into the tube to make it more substantial. Trim off any newspaper sticking out. Press in about 1½in (4cm) for the neck at one end and about 4in (10cm) for the tail at the other, and bind with sticky tape. Bend the joined tubes as shown in the illustration below. They will stay in place when you add the papier-mâché.

Making the Tyrannosaurus rex
3 For the head, thread a needle with strong thread and fasten 1 of the large rollers at right angles to the neck. Stab through the card on one side, take the thread round a wire in the roller, tie the ends and secure. Repeat at the other side.

4 For the front legs, tie three or four of the top coils of one of the narrow rollers together with thread to make it curve.

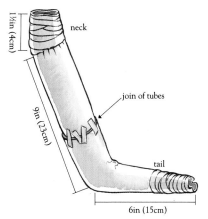

Joining and shaping the cardboard tubes.

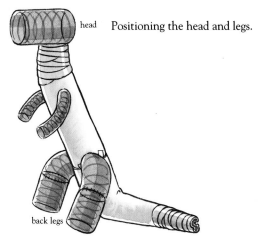

Positioning the head and legs.

Then tie the roller to the body about 2in (5cm) away from the top of the neck as for the head. Repeat for the other front leg.

5 For each of the back legs, tie 2 rollers together end to end and curve the top one by tying coils together as before. Tie them to the body as before about 4in (10cm) lower than the front legs. Adjust their positions so that the model can stand on its tail and back legs as shown below.

6 To cover the body with papier-mâché, tear strips of newspaper, soak them in wallpaper paste (see Better Techniques), and wind them round the shape. Where necessary, you can pad out some parts with crumpled or folded newspaper. For the feet, cut ovals of thin card and push them into the open ends of the tubes, then pad them with crumpled newspaper and secure them with more paper strips. Occasionally stand the dinosaur to make sure it will still balance. Add rolled paper for eyes and folded paper for a warty hide, build up the jaws and snout. Leave the model to dry naturally or put it in a slow oven.

Finishing
7 Give the papier-mâché a coat of white or light coloured emulsion paint, then colour it with craft or poster paints. Stick the beads in place for eyes. Stick patches of coloured foil to the hide.

TWO

Gift dinosaurs

❧

Deinonychus greetings card

This dinosaur roamed in packs and preyed on others with its sharp teeth which are featured in this neat pop-up greetings card.

Materials
Scrap paper
10 × 9in (25 × 23cm) of stiff green paper
Same amount of stiff red paper
White paint
Red and green felt-tipped pens
Adhesive

Preparation
1 Draw the pattern for the body, overleaf, on a piece of scrap paper, including only the 2 dotted lines in the head.

2 Peak fold the paper in half as indicated by the broken line and cut round the outer edge with scissors. With the paper still folded, cut along the upper dotted line in the head for the mouth, and fold along the dotted line below for the jaws. Fold this crease backwards and forwards to sharpen it.

3 Open the paper slightly and push the crease to the other side of the paper, as illustrated to the right. Then close the paper and press it firmly. When you open it again the model should stand with a valley fold down the centre and the lower jaw protruding forwards. To make sharp teeth, refold the paper as in step 2 and serrate the jaw edges with scissors.

Making the greetings card
4 Transfer the pattern to stiff green paper, including all the face markings and repeat steps 1, 2 and 3, first scoring the lengthwise fold. Paint the teeth, claws and eyes white. Outline the claws and eyes, draw on the nose and colour the spaces between the hind legs with green felt-tipped pen. Mark the nostrils and the pupils of the eyes with red felt-tipped pen.

5 Transfer the pattern for the body to stiff red paper, omitting all markings. Score and fold the paper in half down the length and cut round the outline about ⅛in (3mm) away from the edge, keeping the base of the model straight below the claws and the lower edge of the body. Stick the green and red layers together so that the red outline is just visible. Be careful not to stick the lower jaw, so that it will still protrude.

6 Draw the pattern for the arms, overleaf, on a piece of squared paper and cut 2 arms from green stiff paper. Paint the claws white and outline them with green felt-tipped pen. Stick the underneath of the arms to the front of the body at the top only, and bend them forward slightly. You could give the Deinonychus a small card to hold between its front claws to show your name and greeting.

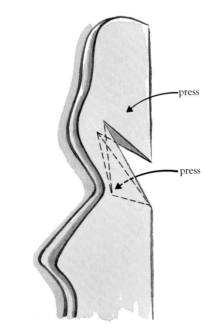

Making the mouth.

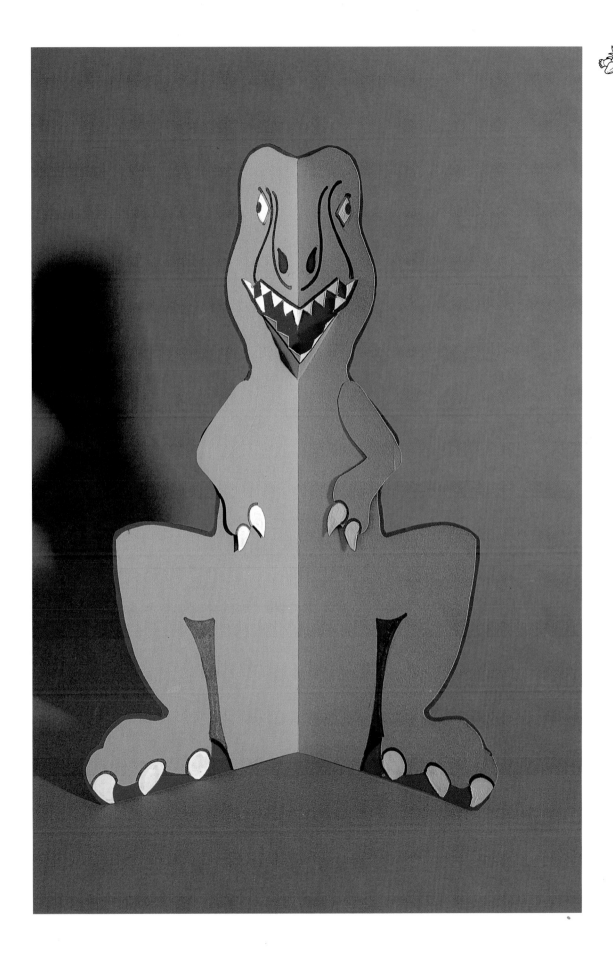

The body pieces.

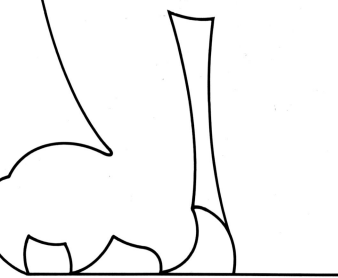

cut

fold

jaws

trace off actual size

fold

BODY

cut 1 in green paper

cut 1 in red paper slightly larger

red base

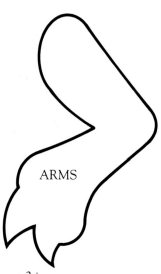

ARMS

cut 2 in green paper

Dimorphodon greetings card

Here is a monster card which will leap out of its envelope to give your friends a real surprise.

Materials
Scrap paper
21 × 12½in (53 × 31cm) dark blue paper
10in (25cm) square of black paper
Red, orange and white paint
Adhesive
Silver marker and/or sequins

Preparation
1 Make a pattern of the Dimorphodon on scrap paper. Rule two squares, one 6½in (16cm) (A) and the other 3¼in (8cm) (B). Label one surface of each square "outside" and the other surface "inside".

2 With the inside of A facing, peak fold, then valley fold it. With the inside of B facing, valley fold it as illustrated to the right. Sharpen the creases and join the two squares carefully together with a piece of sticky tape as shown opposite. Fold them so that you can snip into parts of the edges for teeth.

Making the greetings card
3 Score the blue paper as shown below and fold into half widthways, then fold in half lengthways. With the paper folded, trim the edges evenly.

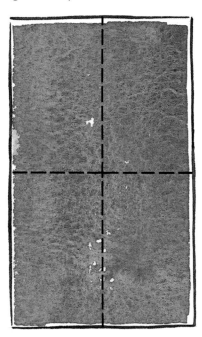

Scoring the blue paper.

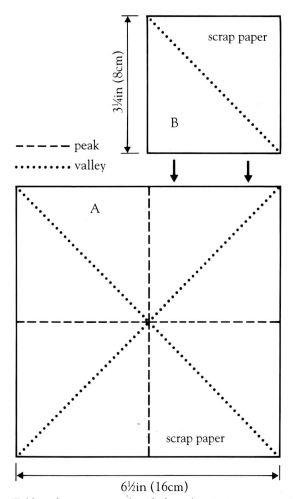

------- peak
········ valley

6½in (16cm)

Folding the scrap paper (inside facing).

4 Transfer the joined Dimorphodon pattern on to black paper and trim off excess. Fold in the same way as the pattern. Paint the shaded parts of the inside red as indicated in the illustration far right.

5 With the inside facing, fold point C up to point D, and bring square B over to the right. This will shape the Dimorphodon. Unfold it and then paint all parts of the teeth white which show when the model is folded.

Finishing
6 Fold square A and stick E to F on both sides together with dabs of adhesive. Bring square B into place and secure invisibly on the inside with sticky tape.

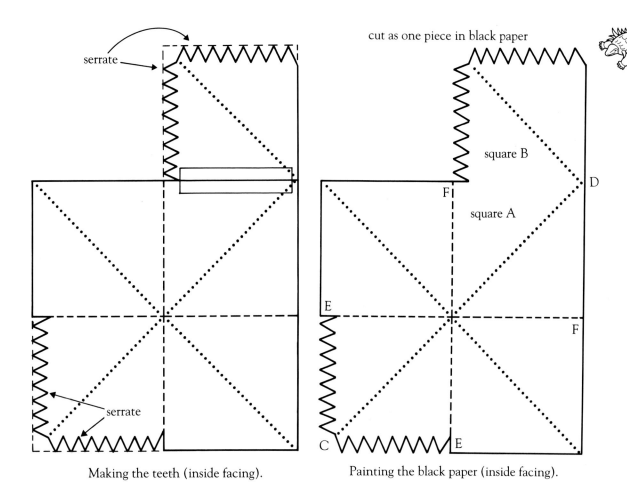

cut as one piece in black paper

serrate

serrate

square B

square A

Making the teeth (inside facing).

Painting the black paper (inside facing).

paint these parts red

7 For the eyes, cut 2 circles ¾in (18mm) diameter and paint them orange, cut 2 circles ½in (12mm) diameter and paint them red with black centres. Stick the orange circles to either side of the head and stick the red circles to one side of the orange ones.

8 Trace the pattern for legs and arms below and cut 2 of each from surplus black paper.

Stick them, underlapping the back of the model, and paint white claws.

9 Add light dabs of adhesive to the back and stick the model into the inner fold of the blue paper. The card should fold flat. Add some stars to the inside with the silver marker and/or sequins.

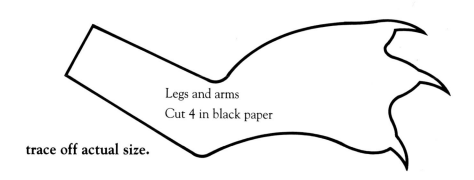

Legs and arms
Cut 4 in black paper

trace off actual size.

37

Triceratops box

This box is very effective and it is easy to make. It is joined throughout with wood glue instead of nails and features a very simple fabric hinge.

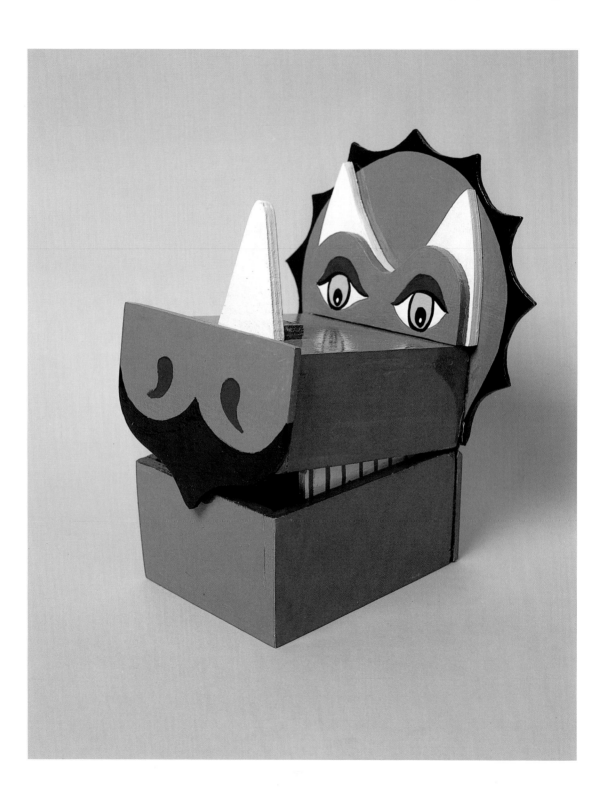

Pieces for the Triceratops box.

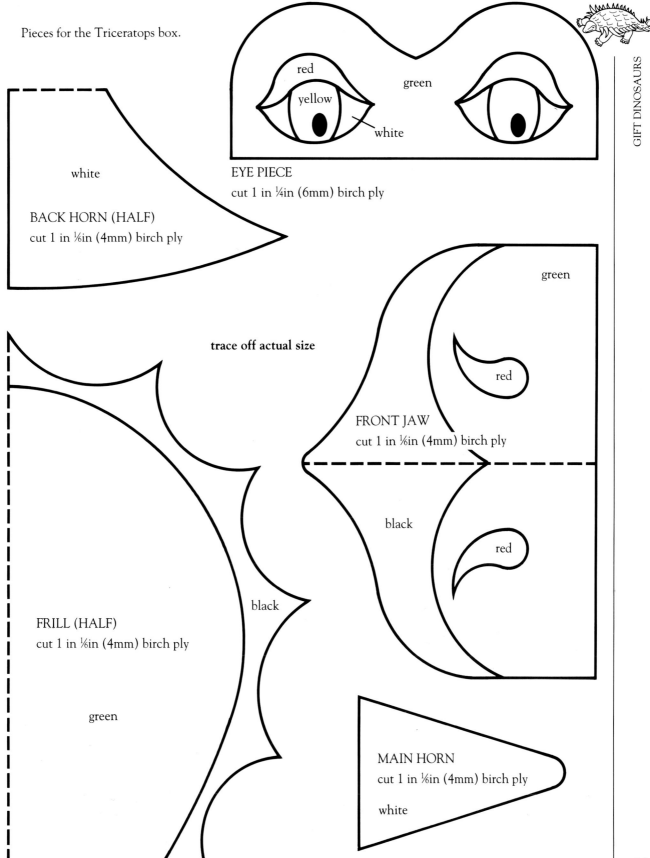

red

yellow

green

white

EYE PIECE

cut 1 in ¼in (6mm) birch ply

white

BACK HORN (HALF)

cut 1 in ⅛in (4mm) birch ply

green

red

FRONT JAW

cut 1 in ⅛in (4mm) birch ply

black

red

trace off actual size

black

FRILL (HALF)

cut 1 in ⅛in (4mm) birch ply

green

MAIN HORN

cut 1 in ⅛in (4mm) birch ply

white

Materials

Thin cardboard
10 × 14in (25 × 36cm) of ¼in (6mm) birch
   ply
10 × 12in (25 × 30cm) of ⅛in (4mm) birch
   ply
4 × 4¾in (10 × 11cm) polyester ribbon or
   similar strong fabric
Four 9mm long screws
Undercoat
Enamel paints in green, red, black, white,
   yellow
Wood glue

Preparation

1 Draw the pattern pieces on thin
cardboard from the patterns on the
previous page. Add the outlines for the frill,
front jaw and eye piece. (Tip: If you are
working in metric, dressmaking squared
paper stuck on thin card ensures correct
measuring and accurate right angles for all
straight pieces.)

2 Cut from ¼in (6mm) birch ply:
For lower part:
2 sides each 2 × 4½in (5 × 11cm)
front and back each 2 × 3½in (5 × 9cm).
For upper part:
2 sides each 1½ × 4½in (4 × 11cm)
front and back each 1½ × 3½ (4 × 9cm).
Base and top of box will be cut later
Cut 1 main horn
1 eye piece

3 Cut from ⅛in (4mm) ply:
1 frill
1 front jaw
2 teeth pieces each 1½ × 2¾ (4 × 7cm)
1 double horn
1 back hinge cover 2¼ × 3¾in (5.5 ×
9.5cm).

Making the Triceratops box

4 Sand all pieces lightly. Sand straight edge
of frill and one long side of back hinge to a
slant, so that the box will open easily when
it is assembled.

5 On top and bottom box stick one side
piece to front or back piece in L shape (see
below). Check with try square that sticking
is at right angles and leave to dry.

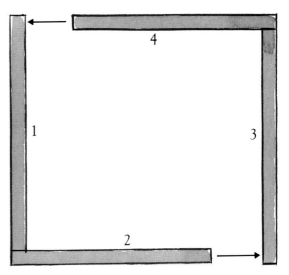

Assembling the sides of the box top and bottom.

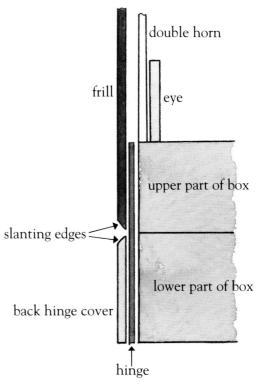

Assembling the back of the box.

6 Stick each L-shaped piece to adjacent piece as shown to the left. Check right angles and leave to dry.

7 Place the assembled box edges for both the upper and lower parts on remaining 6mm ply and draw round outside for top and base. Working in this way ensures fit of top and bottom. Cut out, sand pieces and stick in place.

8 Stick the main horn centrally to top of the box approximately ¾in (18mm) from one end. Cut a support from ¼in (6mm) ply 1¼ × ½in (3 × 1cm). Stick support behind main horn, as illustrated, below.

Painting the teeth pieces.

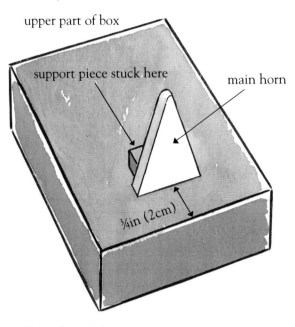

upper part of box

support piece stuck here

main horn

¾in (2cm)

Fixing the main horn.

9 Next comes the painting. First, paint all pieces with undercoat. Then, with the red enamel, paint inside and edges of lower and upper parts of box.
With white, paint both sides and upper edges of main horn, upper edges and one side of double horn.
With green, paint both sides and edges of frill; both sides and edges of front jaw; one side only and upper edges of eye piece; two long sides, one short side and base of lower part of box; long sides only and top of upper part of box; one side only and edges of back hinge cover.
Paint teeth pieces red and white as shown in the illustration, above. Paint the front of the frill black as indicated in the graph pattern.
Also paint features as indicated in the pattern.

10 Assembly (see illustration, opposite). When sticking together, scratch adjacent surfaces a little to give added purchase to wood glue. Place top and bottom of box together. Stick hinge fabric to back of box, leave to dry. Stick back hinge cover over hinge at back of lower part of box, placing straight long edge level with base of box. Stick frill over hinge at top of box. Drill pilot holes and insert 2 screws evenly into edge of frill and 2 into edge of back hinge cover, ½in (12mm) above and below join of hinge.

11 Stick front head over front of box, allowing straight upper edge to project for ¼in (6mm) and outer edges to project evenly. Stick double horn over frill at back of upper part of box, and front head over double horn. Stick teeth pieces centrally to long edges of inside of lower part of box, so that red parts match inside of box.

41

Dinattack board game

A pack of fierce Velociraptors and a peaceable plant-eating Anatosaurus are on the same track through the swamps. Who will reach the cave and safety first? Will they all survive?

Materials
Squared paper for pattern
17 × 20in (43 × 50cm) of thin coloured cardboard
Same size of strong white paper
Adhesive
Felt-tipped pens or paints
9in (23cm) square of blue paper
Small pieces of brown and dark green paper
Scraps of thin white cardboard for counters
2 small paper bags
1 dice

Preparation
1 Draw the track pattern on squared paper from the graph pattern on pages 46-7. Include tabs marked V1, V2, V3. Cut out in the white paper. Stick the track on the sheet of thin card.

2 Using a felt-tipped pen, divide the track into sections as shown on the graph pattern. Colour 16 of the sections red and 16 blue. Add the letters A, V1, V2 and V3 as on the graph.

3 Tear pieces of blue paper for the swamps and stick them on the card. Tear a piece of brown paper for the cave and stick in place. Cut 4 pieces of white paper for fords and stick them over the swamps, then paint the fords with wavy blue lines. Draw some clumps of fern on the card, then cut some fern leaves from brown and dark green paper and stick them here and there on the card.

4 Make the counters from scrap card. Cut 27 small squares or 27 circles each 1in (2.5cm) across. Colour 11 blue, 13 red and 3 yellow. Write "A" for Anatosaurus on one blue counter and figures 1-10 on the rest of the blue counters. Write "V1", "V2" and "V3" on three of the red counters and figures 1-10 on the rest of the red counters. Write "LIFE" on each of the yellow counters.

Playing the game
5 Put all the numbered red counters into one of the paper bags, and mark it "VELOCIRAPTOR". Put the numbered blue counters into the other bag and mark it "ANATOSAURUS".

6 The object of the game is to reach the cave and safety first. The player who does this is the winner. Some players may be eliminated during the course of the game.

7 This is a game for 2, 3 or 4 players. If there are 4 players, one is the Anatosaurus and three are the Velociraptors. If there are 2 or 3 players, one is the Anatosaurus and you may decide how many Velociraptors there should be (up to three) and who should move their counters.

8 To start the game, place the three red counters marked V1, V2 and V3 (the Velociraptors) on the board in their marked positions. Place the blue counter marked A (the Anatosaurus) on the first square of the board. The players shake the dice in turn. A Velociraptor must throw a six to start. The player immediately throws the dice again and moves the counter for the number of squares shown on the last throw

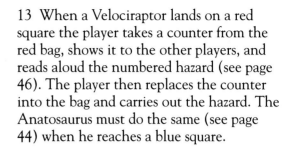

only. The Anatosaurus does not need to throw a six and may begin straight away.

9 In all other dice throws during the game any player who throws a six immediately throws again, then adds together the 2 numbers and moves the counter for the total score.

10 The Anatosaurus takes the 3 yellow counters marked "LIFE". If a Velociraptor and the Anatosaurus occupy the same square at any time the Anatosaurus is injured, and must hand over a "LIFE" counter to the Velociraptor. If he loses all 3 lives he is eliminated.

11 If two Velociraptors occupy the same square, they fight. Both shake the dice in turn. The Velociraptor with the higher score wins the fight and the other Velociraptor is eliminated.

12 The Anatosaurus has much longer legs than the Velociraptors. If he lands on a square connected to a ford he can wade forwards or backwards over it as he wishes. Alternatively, he may remain in the same square if the move would result in danger

from a hungry Velociraptor. Because the Velociraptors would drown, they cannot use the fords.

13 When a Velociraptor lands on a red square the player takes a counter from the red bag, shows it to the other players, and reads aloud the numbered hazard (see page 46). The player then replaces the counter into the bag and carries out the hazard. The Anatosaurus must do the same (see page 44) when he reaches a blue square.

14 Dinosaurs remaining in the game must race each other to reach the cave. A player must throw the exact score needed to get into the cave and win the game.

Hazards for the Anatosaurus

1 If you are attacked while occupying this square you shake off the Velociraptor without having to surrender a life.

2 You fall into a pit. Shake a six to get out.

3 You have just eaten a good meal of leaves. Go forward 3 squares.

4 You must stop to drink. Miss a turn.

5 You attempt to eat a monkey puzzle tree, which makes you ill. Go back 3 squares.

6 You attempt to feed on a conifer, which is difficult to swallow. Go back 2 squares.

7 You suffer bad toothache. Miss a turn while you recover.

8 If you draw this number you can retain it until you are attacked by a

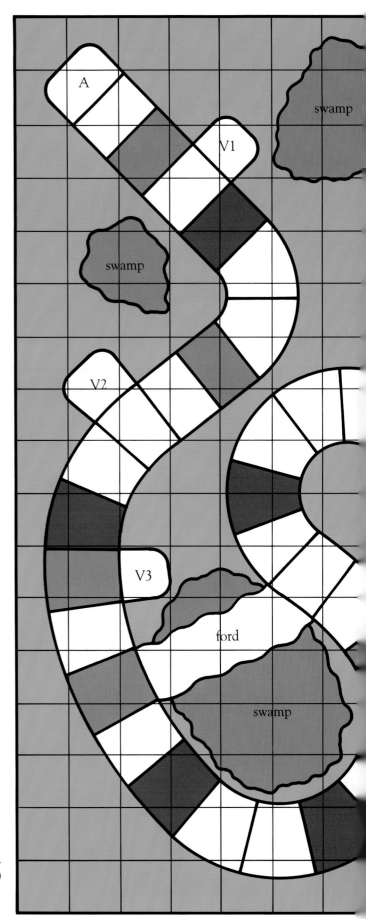

Velociraptor. You manage to stamp on him and do not lose a life. Return the counter to the bag immediately after the fight.

9 You find a short cut. Go forward 4 squares.

10 You take a refreshing mud bath in the swamp. Shake the dice again and add the two scores together for your move.

Hazards for the Velociraptors

1 You fall into a swamp and must shake a six before you can get out.

2 The sun comes out to give you a burst of speed. Shake the dice again and add the two scores together for your move.

3 You are attacked and eaten by a hungry Tyrannosaurus. Leave the game.

4 You climb a tree so that you can see the best way to advance. Go forward 4 squares.

5 A sharp rock damages your tail. Go back 2 squares.

6 If another Velociraptor is waiting to enter the game the player may start without shaking a six. You may choose.

7 Cold nights slow you down. Go back 3 squares.

8 You find a nest of Anatosaurus eggs and stop to eat them. Miss a move.

9 You take a leap from a cliff. Go forward 3 squares.

10 You catch a small early mammal and have a good meal. Go forward 2 squares.

The playing board.
1 square = 1in (2.5cm)

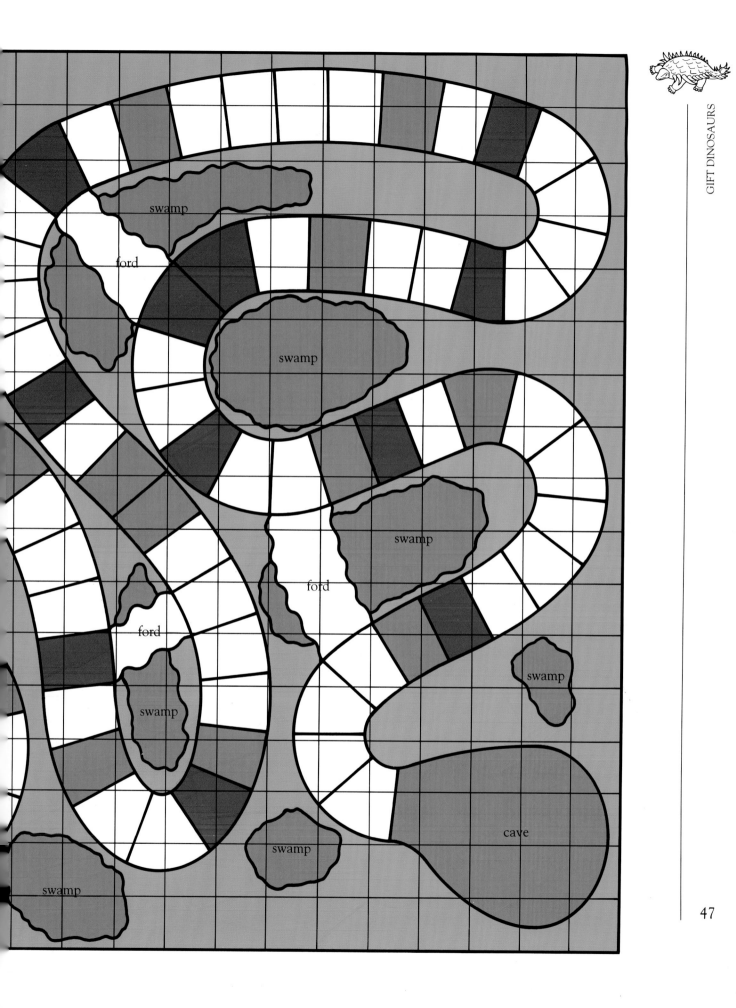

swamp

ford

swamp

swamp

ford

ford

swamp

swamp

swamp

swamp

cave

Windmill

Take this colourful dinosaur outside on a windy day and watch him run!
The stronger the wind, the faster his legs spin round.

Materials
Paper for patterns
8 × 12in (20 × 30cm) of thick cardboard, any colour
4 × 6in (10 × 15cm) of thin white cardboard
8 × 12in (20 × 30cm) cartridge paper
5in (13cm) square of strong coloured paper to match dinosaur
Felt-tipped pens or paints
¾ × 17in (18mm × 43cm) of wood
6in (15cm) of strong galvanized wire
2 wire closers for plastic bags
Adhesive
1 wooden bead ¾in (18mm) diameter
1 small wooden bead

Preparation
1 Draw the dinosaur outline from the graph pattern on pages 52-3 on to squared paper. Transfer the outline only on to thick cardboard. Transfer the same outline but this time with details, including point for hole × added, to cartridge paper. Transfer the pattern for the dinosaur legs (overleaf) 4 times to thin cardboard. Transfer the pattern for the windmill (overleaf) including the 5 points for holes to strong coloured paper. Cut out all pieces.

Making the windmill
2 Colour or paint the dinosaur on cartridge paper as in the photograph opposite. Stick it to the thick cardboard and push a hole through both thicknesses at point × to take the galvanized wire. Colour 1 side only of each leg, making sure that the toes point to the right.

3 Make holes in the windmill where marked and enlarge them carefully with a

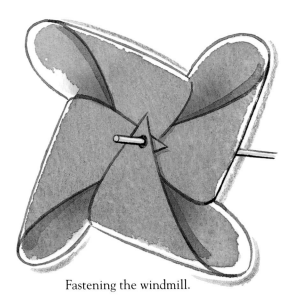

Fastening the windmill.

medium thickness knitting needle point. The holes must fit loosely over the wire to make the windmill revolve.

4 Drill a hole to fit the wire in the centre of the wood 2in (5cm) from one end. Cut a groove across the wood about 1in (2.5cm) below the hole and a nick either side of the wood at the ends of the groove. With the grooved side of the wood facing you push the piece of wire through the hole and bend its far end down at right angles for 1½in (4cm). To fasten the end of the wire against the wood, twist together 2 plastic bag closers end to end, place them in the groove, then twist together the ends of the closers over the end of the wire on the other side of the wood, as illustrated opposite, top.

5 Working from the back of the card, push the free end of the wire through the hole in the dinosaur, and mark the position of the wood on the back of the cardboard. Lift the

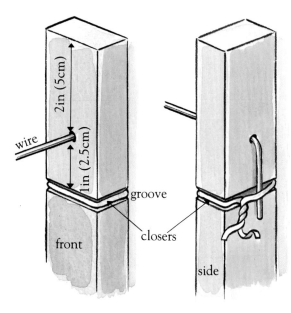

Fixing the wire to the handle.

dinosaur so that you can apply glue to the marked position, then replace it to stick it on to the wood. Push the large bead over the projecting wire.

6 With the windmill placed as illustrated on the previous page, curl the pointed ends in the numbered order given on the pattern right and thread them over the wire, then place the smaller bead on top. Check that the windmill will spin freely, then bend the excess wire over the bead and trim off with pliers close to the bead.

7 Stick the backs of the dinosaur legs to the vanes of the windmill as in the photograph above.

50

The windmill pieces.

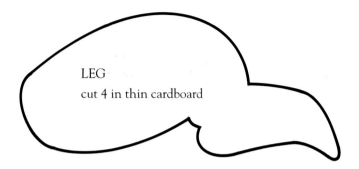

LEG
cut 4 in thin cardboard

trace off actual size

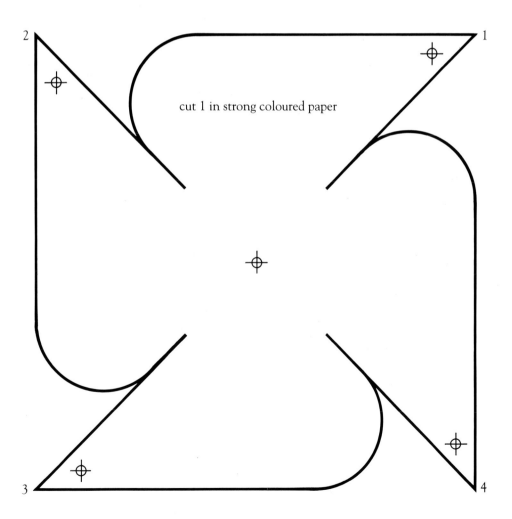

2   1

cut 1 in strong coloured paper

3   4

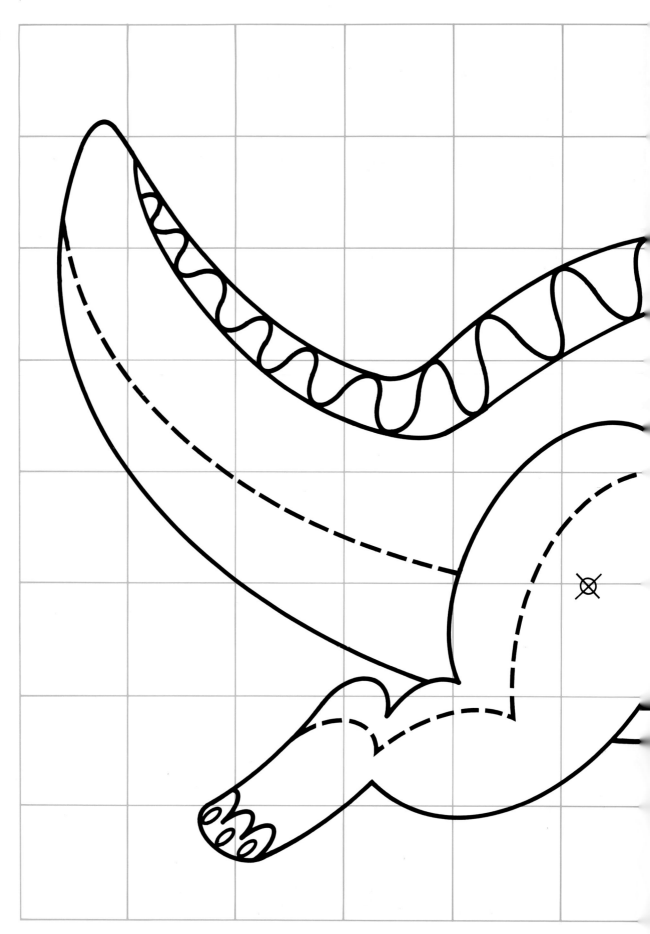

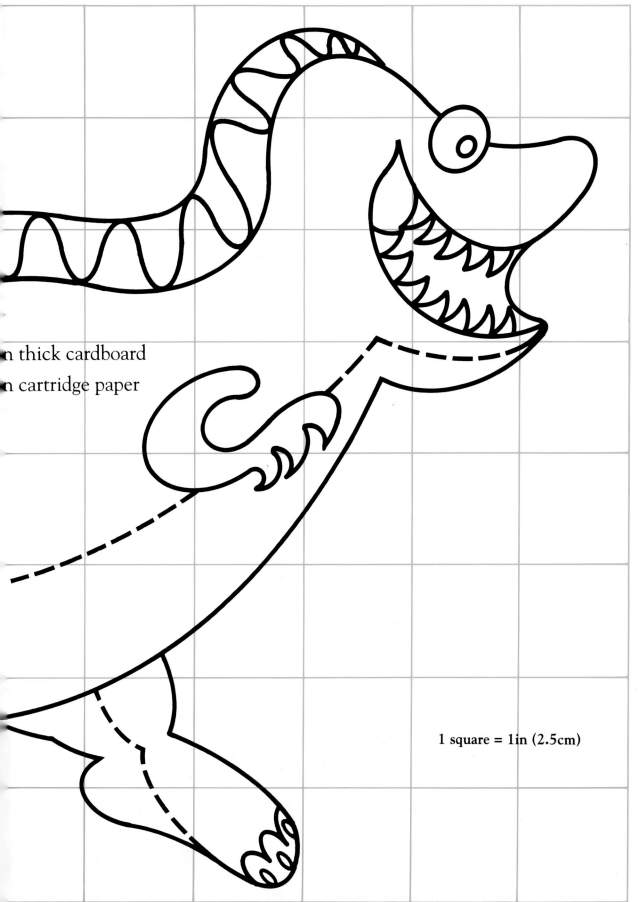

n thick cardboard

n cartridge paper

1 square = 1in (2.5cm)

THREE

Puppets and flying dinosaurs

Brachiosaurus puppet

Here is a puppet easily made by the children. Requiring paper scraps and drinking straws, its cost is next to nothing.

57

Materials

Paper for patterns
Thin scrap cardboard for patterns
A few drinking straws
Discarded greetings cards or stiff, coloured
    magazine covers
Adhesive
Medium thickness white cardboard
Strong thread
Felt-tipped pens
Small play ball, approximately 2in (5cm)
    diameter
Paint to match play ball
2 small joggle eyes
3ft (96cm) of garden cane
Small bead

Preparation

1 From the pattern opposite trace half
patterns for the three scales (A, B and C),
legs and tail. Transfer patterns to folded
thin scrap cardboard placing dotted line to
fold. Cut out all patterns and unfold.

2 Cut 2 or 3 plastic drinking straws into
¼in (6mm) lengths.

Making the puppet

3 Draw round smallest scale A 32 times on
the greetings cards and cut out. Fold each
scale in half as shown by dotted line on
pattern with coloured side outside. Dab a
little glue inside the scale along upper edge,
stick the edges together and leave to dry.

4 Make 18 medium-sized scales B in the
same way and 21 largest-sized C.

5 Cut 2 legs and 1 tail from the white
cardboard and paint both sides of each.
Curve in half but do not fold sharply. Cut 2
lengths of scrap cardboard each
approximately 1 × 6in (2.5 × 15cm). Roll
each strip round a pencil to make tubes and
stick ends in place. Apply adhesive along
each tube and stick them underneath fold
of each leg as illustrated above.

6 Cut off a length of thread about 72in
(180cm) and insert end into a needle.

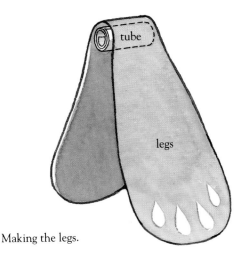

Making the legs.

String a small bead for the puppet's nose
and tie to the end of the thread. Push
needle through centre of play ball. Push
needle through point × on 28 A scales, 8 B
scales and 6 C scales separating each with a
piece of drinking straw. Thread one pair of
legs through its inside tube, then continue
to thread remainder of C scales separating
each with drinking straw pieces. Thread
the second pair of legs, then remainder of B
scales and remainder of A scales. Take
thread through folded top of tail, as
illustrated, previous page. Allow remaining
thread to hang loose for the time being.

Finishing

7 Paint the top of the puppet leaving some
of the pictures on the greetings cards
showing through.

8 Draw a face on the play ball and stick
joggle eyes in place.

9 To control the puppet, drill 2 small holes
in the cane 13in (33cm) from each end.
Drill a further 2 holes at equal distances
between. Take thread from the tail up to
one end of cane, wind round and secure so
that puppet hangs about 12in (30cm)
below cane. For the head string, push
needle through head from top to bottom
and knot firmly to secure under the head,
fasten other end to the opposite end of the
cane. Fasten a thread in the same way in
front of each leg and push each through
corresponding hole in cane.

The body pieces.

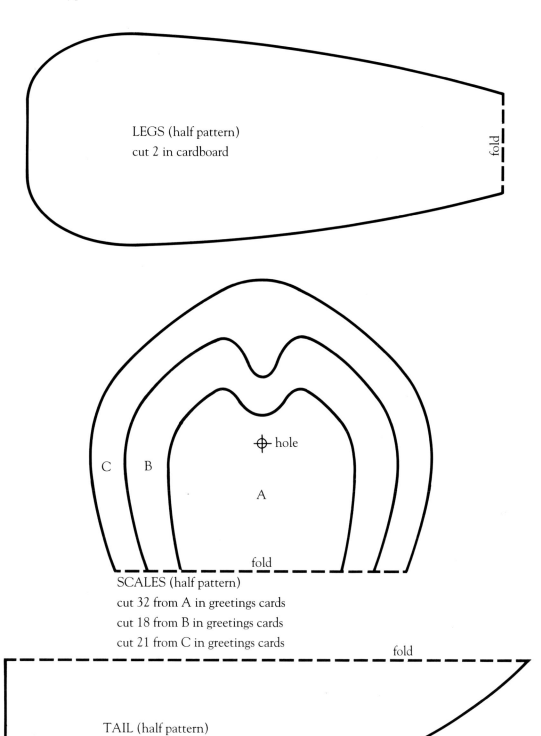

LEGS (half pattern)
cut 2 in cardboard

fold

C   B

⊕ hole

A

fold

SCALES (half pattern)

cut 32 from A in greetings cards

cut 18 from B in greetings cards

cut 21 from C in greetings cards

fold

TAIL (half pattern)
cut 1 in cardboard

Dinosaur baby puppet in his egg

Make the egg easily from papier-mâché and knit the colourful baby.
Then make him hatch from his egg!

Materials
For the baby
1 pair of 3¼mm (No 10) knitting needles
2oz (50g) altogether of assorted green
    shades of double knitting wool
Small quantity of same ply wool in black,
    red, white, orange
Foot of discarded tights
Stuffing
2 shiny black buttons
4 pipe cleaners
For the egg
Balloon
Newspaper
Lining paper
Wallpaper paste
Cardboard circle 6in (15cm) diameter
Emulsion paint
2 small rubber bands
2 spent matches
4 paper fasteners with prongs

Making the puppet

Abbreviations
sts – stitches; st st – stocking stitch (1 row
knit, 1 row purl alternately); tog – together;
k – knit; p – purl; g st – garter stitch (every
row knit); rep – repeat; dec – decrease
(work 2 stitches together); inc – increase
(work into front and back of stitch); tbl –
through back of loop; cont – continue.

Work in random stripes, varying shades of
green. Use 3¼mm (No 10) needles
throughout.

Body and head
With green wool, cast on 52sts. Cont in st
st and work 10½in (27cm) straight ending
with a p row.

Divide for jaw
K 32, turn, cont on these sts for upper jaw.
Work 5 rows straight. Begin shaping.
Row 1: k 14, k 2 tog tbl, k 2 tog, k 14.
Next and every alt row: p.
Row 3: k 13, k 2 tog tbl, k 2 tog, k 13.
Row 5: k 12, k 2 tog tbl, k 2 tog, k 12.
Row 7: k 11, k 2 tog tbl, k 2 tog, k 11.
(26sts)
Row 9: k 2 tog, k 9, k 2 tog tbl, k 2 tog, k 9,
k 2 tog.
Cont to dec as in row 9 until 10 sts remain.
Next row: p. Cast off.

Upper jaw
Return to remaining 20 sts.
Work 2in (5cm) straight, ending with p
row.
Dec 2 sts each end of next and every
following k row until 10 sts rem.
P 1 row, Cast off.

Mouth
With red wool, cast on 10 sts. Cont in st st.
P 1 row.
*Inc 1 st at each end of next and every alt
row until there are 18 sts.*
Next row: p.
When work measures 2in (5cm),** dec 1 st
each end of next and every alt row until
there are 10 sts,**
Next row: p.
Rep from * to *.
Cont straight until work measures 4¾in
(12cm) ending with a p row.
Rep from ** to **. P 1 row, cast off.

Lower jaw controller
With red wool, cast on 12 sts.
Cont straight in st st until work measures
1¼in (3cm). Cast off.

Eyes (make 2)
With white wool, cast on 4 sts. Cont straight in g st until work measures 3in (7.5cm). Cast off.

Eye lids (make 2)
With orange wool, cast on 4 sts. Cont straight in st st until work measures 2in (5cm). Cast off.

Arms
With green wool, cast on 18 sts. Cont straight in st st in random stripes until work measures 2¼in (6cm). Dec 1 st at each end of next 7 rows (4 sts).
Work 4 rows.
Inc 1 st each end of next 7 rows (18 sts).
Work 6 rows.
Dec 1 st each end of next and foll alt row (14 sts).
Work straight for 1¼in (3cm). Cast off.

Finishing the puppet
1 Press work lightly on wrong side. Body: with right sides facing, join long edges to division for jaw. With right sides facing, pin mouth to lower and upper jaw and stitch all round.

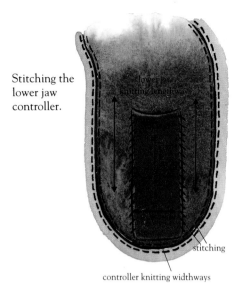

Stitching the
lower jaw
controller.

stitching

controller knitting widthways

2 With right side facing, pin the lower jaw
controller lengthways to the centre of the
wrong side of the lower jaw, as illustrated
above. With small stitches, oversew in
place. It should fit your thumb snugly. Turn
work to right side.

3 To shape top of head, cut off
approximately 2¾in (7cm) from toe end of
foot of tights and stuff lightly. Oversew
opening to close. Insert your fingers into
the top of the puppet's jaw and your thumb
into the lower jaw control. Push the stuffed
tights ball into place from the open end of
the body so that it rests on your knuckles,
and pin it into place from the right side.
Remove your hand from the puppet and
neatly catch the ball of stuffing in place
from the right side using matching sewing
cotton.

4 Embroider a line of chain stitiches in
white round the jaw line and add a few
small "teeth" with fly stitches touching the
line of chain stitches.

5 Eyes: join short ends of eye strip, gather
and draw up one long edge. Oversew eye to
side of head inserting a little stuffing under
it to pad. Add the other eye, then stitch
the buttons firmly to the centres sewing
right through the head. Oversew the
eyelids to the top of each eye and

embroider a line of stem stitches in orange
wool round the bottom of each. Embroider
a chain stitch in red for each nostril.

6 Arms: with right sides facing, join shaped
edges on each side of arm to form darts.
Fold in half lengthways and stitch all
round, leaving space to turn. Pair 2 pipe
cleaners and twist lightly, insert into arm.
Stuff lightly, close opening. Bend the foot
end downwards and embroider divisions in
black wool to mark 3 toes, then embroider
a chain stitch in white wool for the claw at
the end of each. Oversew arms loosely to
the sides of the body approximately 1½in
(4cm) down from division of jaw.

The egg

Preparation
7 Inflate balloon to measure approximately
24in (60cm) circumference and tie neck
securely. Place the balloon in a bowl for
ease of handling.

8 Tear strips of newspaper into pieces
about 1¾in (4cm) square. Do the same with
strips of lining paper.

Making the egg
9 For the first coat of papier-mâché use
water only and moisten the newspaper
thoroughly. Cover the balloon with
overlapping pieces of newspaper. Leave the
neck of the balloon showing throughout.

10 Mix up some thick wallpaper paste. For
the second coat use pieces of wallpaper
lining paper. Add a layer of overlapping
pieces of pasted paper. Continue with layers
of newsprint and plain paper until there are
6 layers in all, ending with plain paper.
Place the balloon on a flat surface with the
tied neck pointing upwards and leave to dry
in a warm place.

11 When the papier-mâché is dry, prick
the balloon at the neck, and when it is
deflated lift it out. Patch over the hole with
more pasted newspaper and leave to dry.

12 Mark a circle with a 3in (7.5cm) diameter on the flattened base of the balloon, where it was standing to dry, and

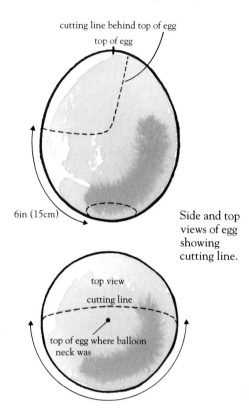

cutting line behind top of egg
top of egg
6in (15cm)
Side and top views of egg showing cutting line.

top view
cutting line
top of egg where balloon neck was

Below: positioning the base rim.

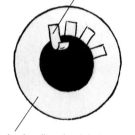

fix in place with pasted pieces of paper
circle of cardboard with hole in centre

Below: Joining sections with rubber bands.

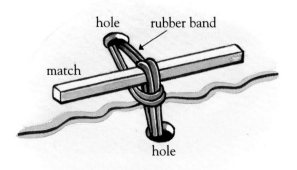

hole   rubber band
match
hole

carefully cut through all layers with a sharp craft knife used in a sawing movement. This is the hole for your arm when you work the puppet.

13 With a tape measure, draw a line half way round the circumference of the balloon 6in (15cm) up from the edge of the hole. Referring to the illustration showing the side view of the egg (left), draw a line over the top of the balloon. Cut along this line making the edges a little irregular.

14 For the base, cut a circle of medium weight cardboard with a 6in (15cm) diameter and a 3in (7.5cm) hole in the centre. With more pasted pieces of newspaper, fix this over the hole in the bottom of the egg (see illustration, left). You will need this base to steady the egg with your other hand as you manipulate the puppet.

15 Paint the inside and outside of the egg and its base.

16 To joint the top of the egg and the loose section, pierce two holes about 1¼in (3cm) apart in the egg, ½in (12mm) from edge, and 2 corresponding holes in egg section. Pull a doubled rubber band through matching holes to outside of egg to fasten pieces together. The easiest way to do this is to loop a small piece of fine wire round the rubber band and push the wire through a hole from the inside of the egg. Then pull the looped band partially through the hole with pliers. Slip a spent match through each looped band to hold it in place (see illustration, left).

Finishing

17 Place the puppet inside the egg and bring the end of the body through the hole to the outside of the base. Insert 4 pronged paper fasteners at regular intervals through the knitting and the base to hold the puppet in place. Paint the knitting showing under the base to match the egg.

Flying Rhamphorhynchus

Make this flying reptile for plenty of shock-horror as it swoops from your bedroom ceiling.

Materials
Squared paper for patterns
13 × 12½in (33 × 32cm) of corrugated cardboard
Strong black plastic rubbish bag
Impact adhesive
Black gloss paint
Red and white gloss or emulsion paint
2 egg sections cut from cardboard egg box as one piece
2 round black buttons
26 spent matches
2 wooden coat hangers
Newspaper
Thick wallpaper paste
9 pipe cleaners each 6½in (17cm)
Strong black cotton
Black fabric 2½ × 4in (6 × 10cm)
30in (74cm) of round black elastic

Preparation
1 Draw the pattern pieces on squared paper from the graph pattern overleaf. Cut the head 3 times and the tail once from corrugated cardboard. Cut the wings twice from black plastic.

Making the Rhamphorhynchus
2 For the head, stick the head pieces together. Stick pasted strips of newspaper on both surfaces and over the edges to neaten them. Fold the head in half over a ½in (12mm) diameter round handle and leave to dry, then push a hole in the centre back fold to take the end of one coat hanger.

3 Paint the outside of the head with black gloss paint and the inside with red emulsion. Paint a narrow line of white emulsion ½in (12mm) from the edges of the inside for the base of the teeth.

4 For the teeth, stick the spent matches into a potato for ease of handling and paint them white. When dry, cut them in half. Using a bradawl or scissors point, push equally-spaced shallow holes along the line painted for the teeth base and stick the half matches in place.

5 The eyes are made from the cardboard egg sections painted white. Leave to dry, then stick them to the head. Fold and stick a piece of black plastic over the back of the eyes for eyelids. Paint a red circle on the front of the eyes, then stick a button in the centre of each circle.

6 Make a tail as for the head, stick and nail it to the under edge of one end of a coat hanger. Saw 2 nicks in the edge of the hanger 2 and 3½in (5 and 9cm) away from the other end. Stick this end into the prepared hole at the back of the head, as illustrated (below). Paint the body black.

back claw nick 3½in (9cm) away from curved end
tail
head
wing support nick 2in (5cm) away from curved end

Fixing the coat hanger in place.

7 To make the claws, wind pasted strips of newspaper round each pipe cleaner and leave to dry, then cut 7 of them in half. For the front claws, fasten 3 half cleaners together with thread and spread them apart, then wind a layer of pasted

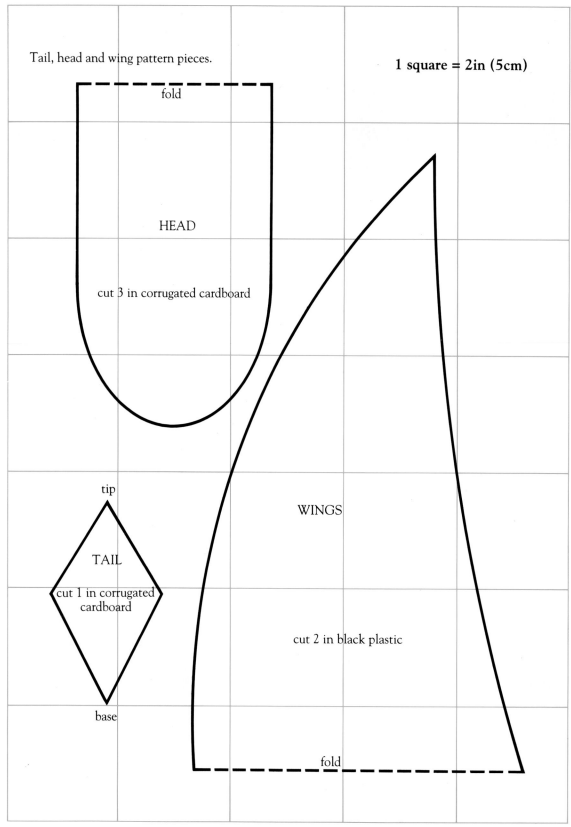

Tail, head and wing pattern pieces.

1 square = 2in (5cm)

fold

HEAD

cut 3 in corrugated cardboard

tip

TAIL

cut 1 in corrugated cardboard

base

WINGS

cut 2 in black plastic

fold

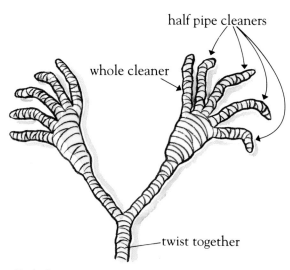

Back claws.

newspaper over the thread. For the back claws, bundle together 1 whole and 4 half cleaners as before, then twist together the ends of the 2 whole cleaners, as illustrated, above. Paint the claws black, then paint the end of each white and tip it with red. Bind the joined back claws to the nick in the body furthest from the head, positioning them on the same edge of the hanger as the tail.

8 For the wing support, drill a small hole ¾in (18mm) away from each end of the other hanger. Saw the hanger in half, then saw deep nicks in both sides of the hanger near the cut ends and similar nicks 2½in (6cm) from each curved end. To make a

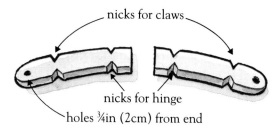

Cutting the coat hanger

hinge between the coat hanger halves, wind the piece of black fabric lengthways round the sawn end of one piece and bind it firmly into the prepared nicks with strong thread (see illustration, below). Insert the other sawn end into the fabric tube and bind it. Fasten a front claw to each of the remaining nicks by sticking and binding them in place. Bind the hinge of the wings to the nick on the body nearest to the head.

9 To attach the wings, smear a little adhesive all over the wing support and stick the upper wing in place. Lift the wing support upwards and stick the under wing to the other side of the support in the same way, enclosing the joined ends of the back claws. Trim the wings as necessary.

Finishing

10 Tie the black elastic round the body just in front of the tail. Tie the other end temporarily to the body just behind the head. Take a length of black thread through each of the holes at the ends of the wing support. Hold the puppet by the thread ends and the elastic so that it tips forward and fasten them all together. You may find it will balance better if the front end of the elastic is taken through the top of the head and knotted. Hang the puppet from a loop of thread or a curtain ring.

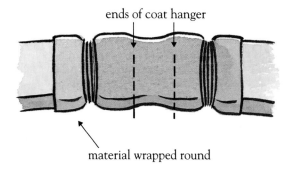

Making the hinge

Archaeopteryx

Archaeopteryx was the first flying bird-like reptile. This one will spread its wings every time you remember to hang up your coat.

Materials
Squared paper for patterns
12 × 16in (30 × 40cm) of ¼in (6mm) birch ply, with grain running lengthways
9 × 9in (23 × 23cm) of ⅙in (4mm) birch ply
Sandpaper
1 dolly peg or 1½in of ⅝in diameter dowel (4 × 1.5cm)
Wood glue
Five ⅝in (18mm) countersunk brass screws
1½in (4cm) of ¼in (6mm) dowel
Craft paints
Clear varnish
1 brass mirror holder 1¼in (3cm) wide
Strong polyester button thread

Preparation
1 Draw the pattern pieces on squared paper from the graph pattern overleaf. Include outline of centre slot and pivot points A and B, and thread holes C.

2 Grain should run lengthways on each piece. Transfer pattern for body twice on to ¼in (6mm) birch ply. Mark pivot points A and slot on one body. Mark pivot points only on the other. Transfer pattern for wings twice on ⅙in (4mm) birch ply. Mark pivot points B and thread holes C on each.

Making the Archaeopteryx
3 Cut out wings and body using a coping or fret saw, or a jig saw if you have one. Cut slot. Clamp body pieces firmly together and drill ¼in (6mm) wide holes at A through both pieces together, to ensure they line up correctly.

4 Clamp wings likewise and drill ⅓in (8mm) holes at B and small holes at C for thread. Sandpaper all pieces, including edges.

5 Cut slider from ⅙in (4mm) birch ply ¾ × 6in (18mm × 15cm). Drill a small hole for thread close to each corner on one short end. Cut off prongs of dolly peg. Stick dolly peg or ⅝in (1.5cm) diameter dowel to centre of one side of slider. When the glue is dry insert a screw into centre of peg from the other side of the slider.

6 For spacers, cut 2 pieces of 6mm birch ply each 1⅜ × 2in (3.5 × 5cm), and 2 strips of same ply each ¼ × 1½in (6mm × 4cm). Cut ¼in (6mm) diameter dowel into 2 pieces each ¾in (2cm) long for pivots.

7 Stick pivots into holes A to project at back of body with slot. Working on back of same piece stick spacers as shown in illustration, overleaf. Ensure that slider will move easily between the edging strips.

8 Paint and varnish fronts of body and wings, ensuring that you have a pair. The wings must be very smooth and their holes remain clear.

Finishing
9 To string the slider, push peg from the back of the body through slot. Slide it to the top of the slot (see illustration, overleaf). Working on reverse of front body, place wings in fully dropped positions over pivot dowels. Insert thread into a needle and double it. Push needle through one hole at top corner of slider and through adjacent hole C at top of wing. Knot thread to form a loop retaining wing and slider as first placed. Loop the other wing in the

same way. Add adhesive to secure the knots and cut thread about ½in (12mm) from them.

10 Place body back in position over pivots. Insert 2 screws to fasten it over lower space. Screw the mirror hanger at the top of the head into the upper spacer.

Fixing the spacers and pivots in place.

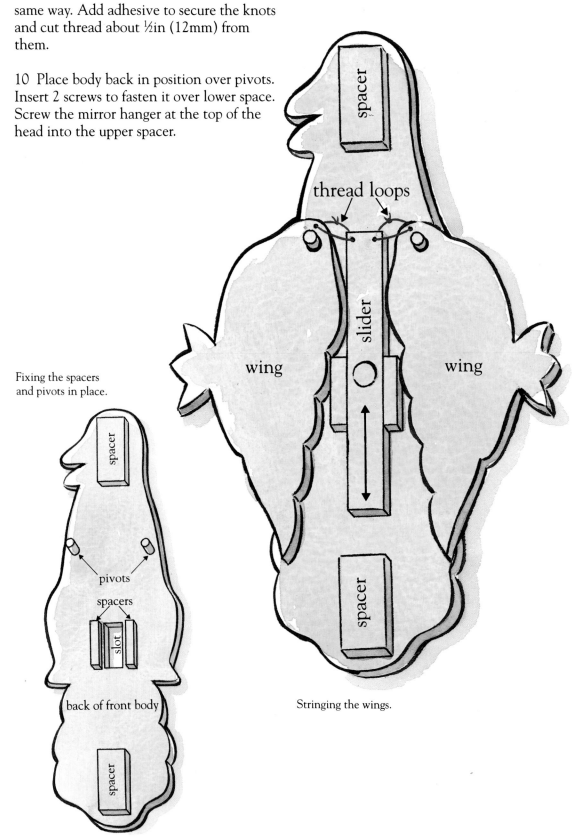

Stringing the wings.

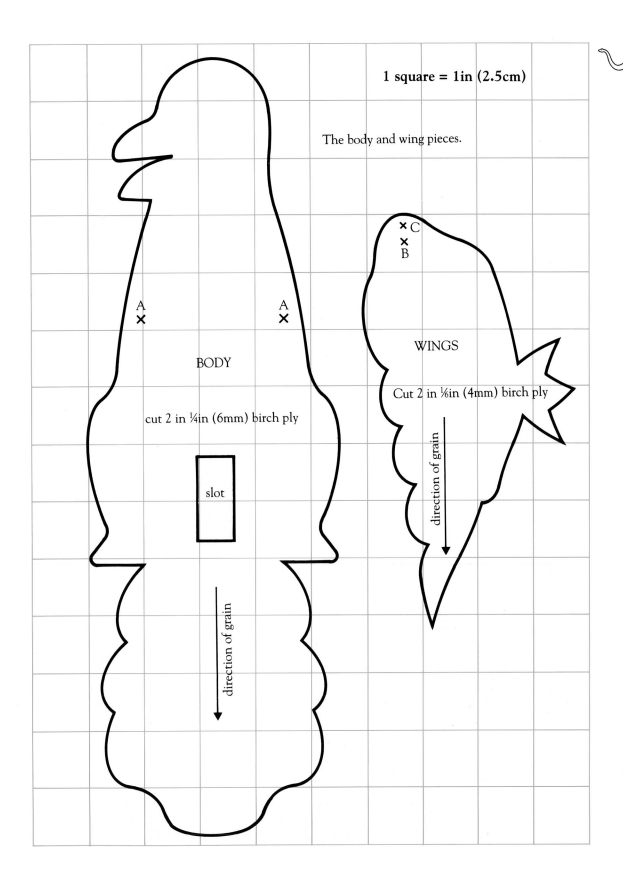

1 square = 1in (2.5cm)

The body and wing pieces.

×C
×B

×A   ×A

WINGS

BODY

Cut 2 in ⅛in (4mm) birch ply

cut 2 in ¼in (6mm) birch ply

slot

direction of grain

direction of grain

FOUR

Decorative dinosaurs

Dino stencils

Dino stencils can decorate lampshades, book jackets, T-shirts or walls, to name a few! Scale them up or down for a variety of effects.

Materials
Paper for pattern
Scrap of washable wallpaper
Masking tape or repositionable spray glue
Stencil card
Cutting board
Scalpel or craft knife
Stencil brushes in sizes to suit design
Craft or poster paints
Paper for book jacket or lampshade

Preparation
1 Either trace the designs overleaf on to thin paper or photocopy them, scaling as you wish.

2 If you are unused to stencil cutting try out one of the designs using a scrap of washable wallpaper. Coat the back of your tracing or photocopy with spray glue, and position it on the washable side of the wallpaper.

Working the design
3 Stick the tracing or photocopy lightly on the stencil card and cut through both layers. Use the cutting board, or a piece of hardboard padded with several layers of newspaper as a protection for your table (see Better Techniques).

4 Practise stencilling on scrap paper to help you decide on the colours you are going to use, and the technique of stencilling. It is essential to stencil with clean, dry brushes.

5 When you are ready to begin, mark the positions of your stencils very lightly on the lampshade with a pencil, so that they are spaced correctly. Tape down the edges of the first stencil. As you work, it will help if you support the lampshade from underneath with a curved object, such as a bottle.

6 Apply the paint with an almost dry brush. Mix the colour on a clean saucer, then dip the tips of the bristles in the paint. Dab the brush smartly a few times on a piece of scrap paper. The technique is to print the paint rather than stroke it into the spaces of the stencil.

7 To achieve a solid colour, go over the same area more than once. This is more effective than trying to overload the brush with colour, which may result in the colour running under the stencil.

8 The design can be shaded very effectively. First apply one colour over the area to be shaded. When it is dry, apply the highlight or lowlight from the edge of the stencil inwards.

9 If necessary, paper, as used for the book jacket, can be protected with a light spray of matt varnish.

A Dinosaur Party
Why not have a party with dinosaurs as its theme? You can stencil these patterns on to paper plates and cups (ensure you use non-toxic crayons) and decorate a room by stencilling enlarged versions of the dinosaurs on to lining paper or thin cardboard. Then cut them out and hang them up.

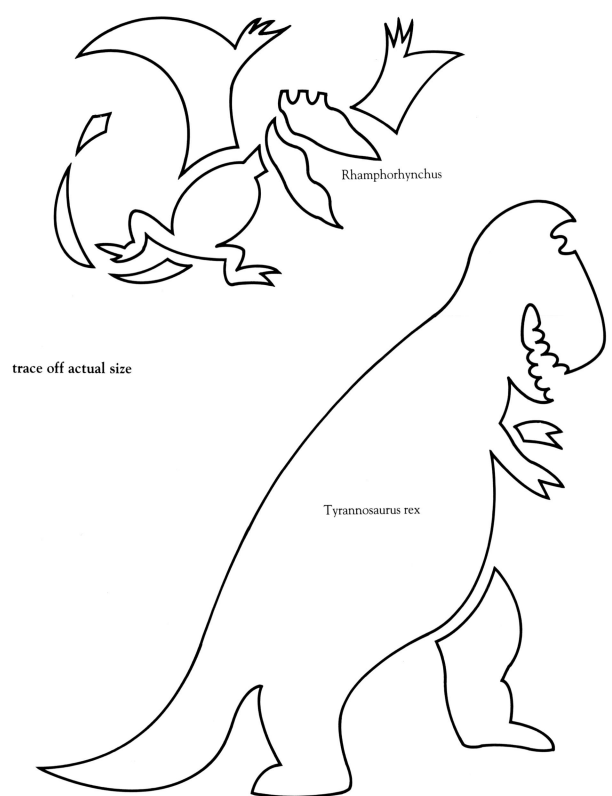

Rhamphorhynchus

trace off actual size

Tyrannosaurus rex

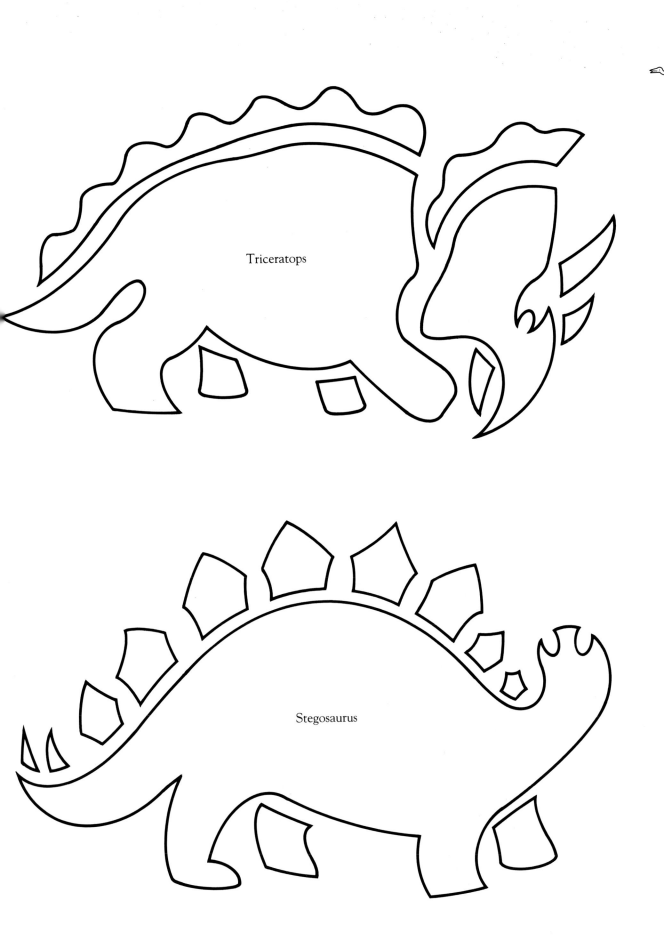

Triceratops

Stegosaurus

Ankylosaurus T-shirt

Colour this fun Ankylosaurus on the front of a white T-shirt using fabric paint and extraordinary puff paint or make a picture for your wall.

Materials
Squared paper
Sheet of white paper same size as design
Black felt-tipped pen
Sheet of scrap cardboard a little larger than design
Fabric painting pen in green, orange and blue
Black puff paint

Preparation
1 Wash, rinse and dry the T-shirt. Iron it flat using a cool iron.

Making the stencil
2 Draw the dinosaur on squared paper from the graph pattern opposite. Transfer the design to a sheet of white paper and draw the outlines in black felt-tipped pen. Stick the design face up lightly to the scrap cardboard.

3 Position the design under the front of the T-shirt and pin the T-shirt over the design, making sure it stays flat.

4 Draw the design on the fabric, following the colours in the photograph below.

Outline the design with black puff paint, keeping the nozzle just above the fabric. Allow the paint to dry thoroughly (see Better Techniques).

Finishing
5 Remove the backing and cover the reverse of your design with a clean cloth.

Iron the painted area gently for 1 minute on a hot setting so that the puff paint will fluff up. Do not press too hard.

6 Do not wash the T-shirt for at least 72 hours. When ironing it, do not iron directly on the design or the puff paint may lift from the fabric and stick to the iron.

1 square = 1in (2.5cm)

Dino jeans

Bright motifs for a variety of effects! Work them as appliqués or simple embroidery: their size can be varied to suit.

Materials

For all five motifs:
Squared paper
Paper for patterns
Garment or background fabric
18 × 24in (46 × 60cm) of fusible web
6 × 14in (15 × 35cm) of cotton fabric
    for largest motif (in this case,
    Tyrannosaurus rex)
7 × 8in (18 × 20cm) of cotton fabric
    for smallest motif (in this case,
    Dimetrodon)
Several assorted pieces of cotton fabric
    in intermediate sizes
Oddments of cotton embroidery thread

Preparation

1 Draw the dinosaur body pieces on squared paper from the patterns on pages 82-5. Draw the legs of each dinosaur separately. Draw the complete body and head in one piece, as indicated by the dotted line under the legs. Include details on the body.

Making the motifs

2 For each motif, cut the whole body and head in one piece, excluding the legs. Cut the legs, head, and any other details separately.

Tyrannosaurus rex

3 Using main colour cotton fabric for the whole body, excluding the legs, place fusible webbing adhesive side down on the wrong side of the fabric. Draw round the pattern for the body on the fusible webbing paper backing. Take care to reverse your design. Cut round the outline, then peel off the paper backing. Place the motif on the garment and fuse it in place by either ironing with hot iron set to steam, or cover with a damp cloth and press with a hot dry iron (see Better Techniques). Leave to cool.

4 Cut the paper pattern round the outline of the contrast front of the dinosaur. Using this separated piece as a pattern, cut and apply the dinosaur front in the same way as you did the body.

5 Last, apply the legs and the arm. Embroider the teeth in blanket stitch and the claws in detached chain stitch. The eyes are worked in stem or satin stitch, with french knots for the black pupils.

Brachiosaurus

6 Apply the lower edge of the body below the pocket line as indicated on the pattern. Work the eye as for the Tyrannosaurus and add a cluster of leaves in detached chain and stem stitch protruding from each mouth.

Dimetrodon

7 Apply the back spikes on top of the main colour body, then apply the legs. Work the eye, teeth and claws as for the Tyrannosaurus.

Triceratops

8 Apply the head on top of the main colour body. The horns can be either applied or embroidered in stem or satin stitch. Apply the legs on top of the body. Work the outline of the mouth and snout in stem or running stitch, and the eyes and claws as for the Tryannosaurus. Work the outline of the back of the head where it overlaps the body in running stitch, as indicated on the pattern.

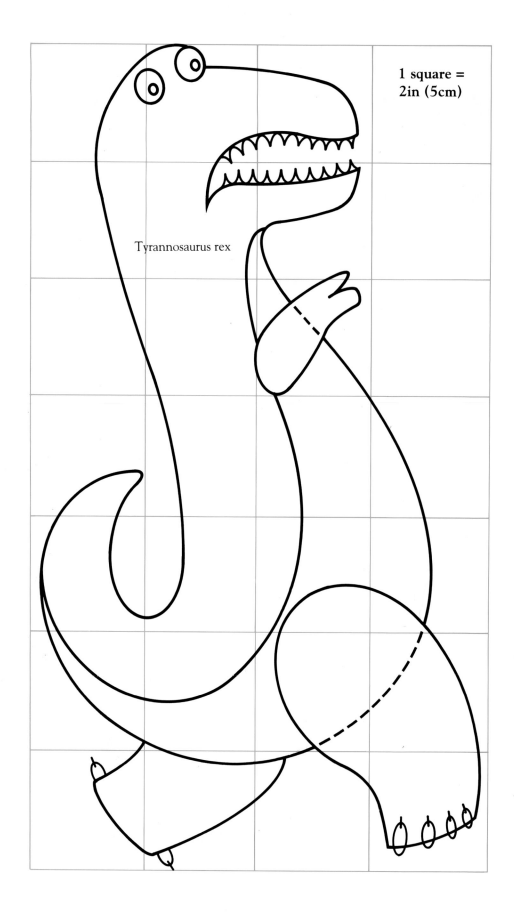

1 square =
2in (5cm)

Tyrannosaurus rex

The dinosaur motifs.

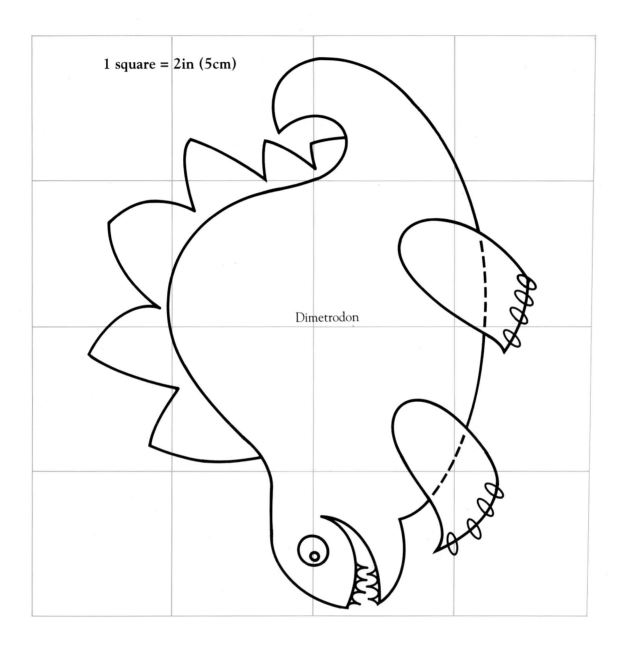

1 square = 2in (5cm)

Dimetrodon

1 square = 2in (5cm)

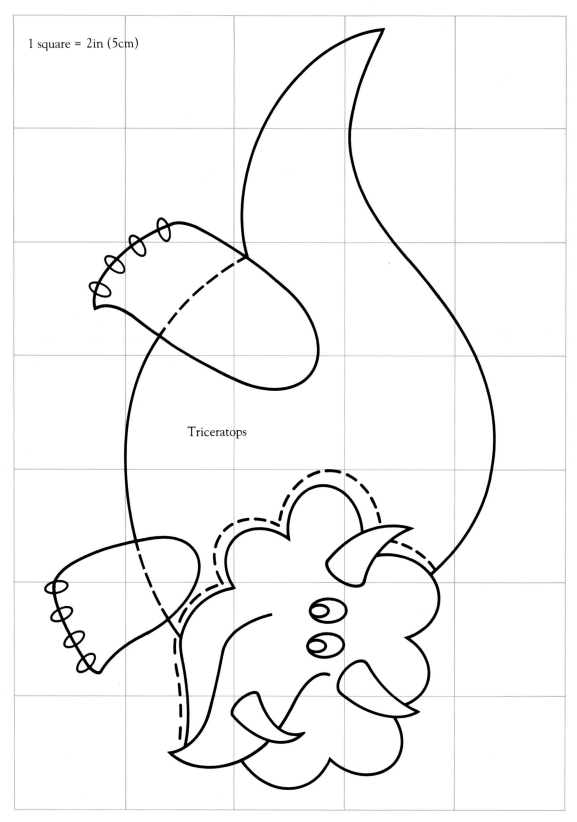

Triceratops

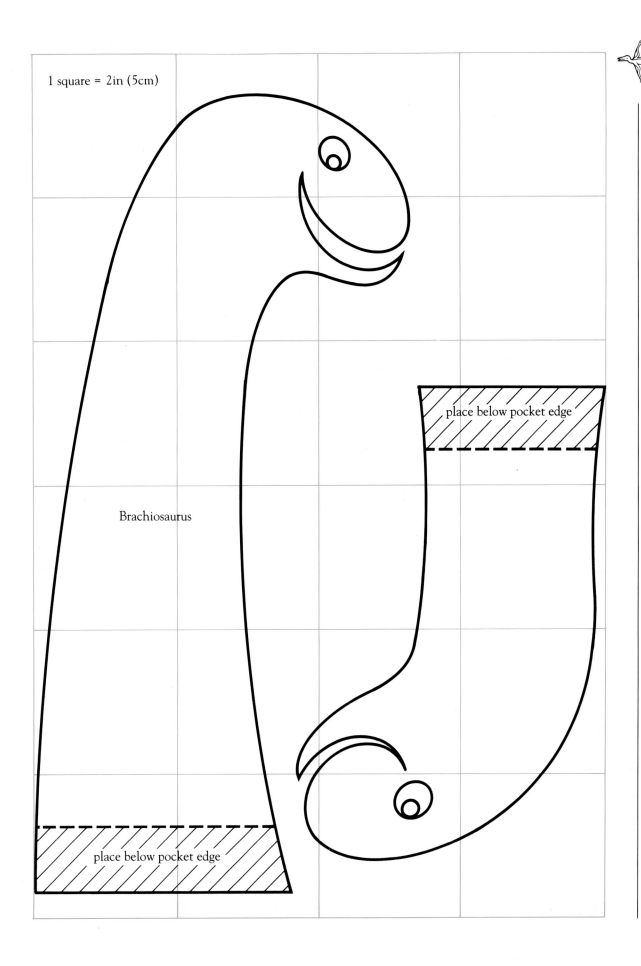

1 square = 2in (5cm)

Brachiosaurus

place below pocket edge

place below pocket edge

FIVE

Better techniques

STENCILLING

Stencilling is one of the simplest decorative techniques. It is inexpensive and stylish. It can be used on walls, paper, fabrics and wood with equal ease.

The dinosaur stencils are given as trace off patterns for you to try this craft. Enlarge the patterns to the size you require for a single motif or a repeat for a border. A photocopier which will enlarge in any proportion is an invaluable help.

Basic equipment

Stencil card

The best stencil card is made specially for the purpose and is heavily impregnated with linseed oil, which makes it durable and waterproof. For practice, a useful substitute for stencil card is a spare piece of washable wallpaper, used with the right side facing you.

Cutting mat

For ease of working, it is worth investing in a double-sided cutting mat. These have the advantage that they "recover" after cutting on them so that they last quite a long time. Alternatively, use a piece of hardboard and pad it well with several layers of newspaper.

Cutting knife

The best cutting tool is small craft knife with a long, straight, pointed blade marked into sections. As the blade becomes less sharp the top section can be snapped off with pliers, leaving the next section ready for use.

Stencil paints

The type of paint you use depends on the surface you are decorating. For paper, use poster paints or acrylic paints of any kind. For walls or wooden surfaces, use the special emulsion paints which are sold in small jars and called craft paints.

For quick results try car spray paints. You may like to experiment with these. They dry quickly and have a good colour range. It is important to keep your work room well ventilated, and you should also wear a special protective mask over your nose and mouth. Practise on a spare piece of paper, applying the paint in light puffs, which are far more effective than more continuous coating. The paint jet can be directed by curling a spare piece of paper round the area you are spraying. It is also necessary to mask off other parts of the design with scrap pieces of paper taped in place around the stencil, otherwise the spray tends to drift beyond the edges of the stencil and on to the surface being stencilled.

Stencil brushes

These come in several sizes and have short, stubby heads. Buy two or three sizes for your first project: a large brush for the main design areas, a smaller brush for the medium-sized areas and a finer brush for details. If you can afford it, more than one brush in each size is very helpful. You can then use a separate brush for each colour without having to continually wash and dry them.

Other equipment

You will also need tracing paper, masking tape, pencils, small foil containers and a roll of kitchen paper. A repositionable spray adhesive is also very useful for keeping the stencils in place.

STENCILLING TECHNIQUES

Transferring the design
Trace the design on to tracing paper. Spray the back of the design with adhesive and place it right side up on to the stencil card or the practise wallpaper. Alternatively, fasten it securely in place with paper clips.

Cutting the stencil
Hold the cutting tool like a pencil. You will find it helpful to stand and bend over your work while you are cutting. In this position it is easier to move your arm from the shoulder, which will help you to cut more smoothly.

Start in the centre of the design and insert the point of the blade slightly beyond the corner of a shape, then pull the knife towards you. Cut as far as you can in one movement, then remove the tool. Begin cutting again, always drawing the blade towards you.

If you are cutting in a circle, leave the point of the blade in place and rotate the stencil with your left hand while you continue the cut. Remove cut sections as you work.

Stencil designs have "bridges" between them to separate colours and to retain the stencil's rigidity. If a bridge is accidentally cut and falls out it can be repaired with a tiny sliver of stencil card stuck in place with a colourless adhesive.

Preparing to paint
Pour a little paint into a small receptacle – a foil container is ideal. Mix it with a thin wooden stick to an even consistency. Poster paints can be used straight from the jar.

Applying the colours
It is important that the stencil is firmly attached to the surface you are going to decorate. For paper, walls or woodwork, the best way to do this is to use a repositionable spray adhesive. Spray the reverse of the stencil, then press it on to the surface to be decorated. The stencil can be moved several times before you need to respray it.

Attach the stencil with strips of masking tape if you are decorating something, such as a fabric lampshade, that might be spoilt by the light film of glue that a spray

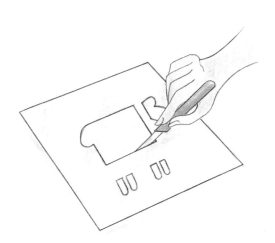

adhesive may leave. The surface of a lampshade may also be pressed in when stencil paint is applied with a brush, so as you work you will need to support it from underneath by something such as a round bottle.

If you are stencilling just one small motif you may be able to hold it in place with your fingers.

Dip the tip of the brush into paint, then dab the brush up and down on a pad of kitchen paper until it is almost dry. Hold it as you would a pen and start at the outer edges of a cut hole. Work round the edges, transferring paint with an up and down dabbing movement of the brush. Move towards the centre of the area. Let the paint dry a little before you apply any shading or other colour to the same place with a clean, dry brush. When all the design is finished, gently lift off the stencil.

Finishing your work

If you have used a spray glue, leave the back of the stencil to dry thoroughly overnight before you put it away. Stencilling on paper which will be handled, such as a book cover, will benefit from a light spray of matt varnish, as will any other surface which needs to be continually wiped.

WOODWORK DETAILS

If you are a complete beginner in woodwork you should still be able to make the toys in this book. For help, encouragement and easy access to tools you could not do better than join a woodwork class at your local evening institute.

Basic Tools

Tenon saw and coping saw or jig saw
Try square
Screw driver
Drill
Two or three clamps in various sizes
Various bits and countersinking bit
Wood glue
Glasspaper in various grades
Sharp HB pencil

A strong table or work bench

Mechanical aids

While it is possible to make simple things in wood using the minimum of tools, one or two mechanical aids will make the work much easier. A hand-held jig saw will not be expensive. These are available with a variety of detachable blades, each suitable for the type of wood you are cutting. The handbook which comes with the tool will give details.

A finishing sander will also save you hours of work. These are available with a variety of grades of glasspaper and will give a beautiful finish to the work.

An extra fine finish can be given to wood if, when you have finished the final sanding, you wet the work thoroughly with clean water and leave to dry. You will then find that the grain has been raised. A final sanding with fine grade glasspaper will give a silky smoothness, ideal for painting or for coating with varnish. If you are painting, rub the paint down between coats of paint for a lovely smooth finish.

Using a try square

An essential tool is a try square, which is needed to ensure that all joints and edges are cut at right angles. It is also useful for checking that everything will fit together well when the work is complete.

Before starting any woodwork it is essential that you should mark the face side and the face edge of the wood. This is the surface that will show when the work is finished. When taking any check with the try square, its wooden handle should always be laid against the face side of the wood.

Work bench

A strong table or folding work bench is essential for woodwork and wherever possible work should be clamped to the bench, using a bit of a scrap wood under the metal pad of the clamp so that it will not crush and mark your work.

Using a tenon saw

When cutting wood with a tenon saw, mark the cutting line on the face side of the wood, then lay the wooden handle of the try square along the face side to mark the cutting line, first on one edge and then on the other. Finally, mark the back of the wood and shade off the waste part which is to be cut away.

Cuts are always made on the waste side of the marked lines so that the thickness of the saw will not cut away part of the shape you are making. Start the cut by placing your left thumb against the saw blade and make a light cut to begin, then begin sawing along the whole length of the saw blade. If the saw blade will not move smoothly, try stroking a spare bit of wax candle along the length of the teeth. Try to keep the saw upright. When the end of the cut is reached, saw very lightly, to avoid the wood breaking off and splintering underneath. You can then check against the marked lines to make sure that you have cut the wood at right angles. If necessary, the edge of the wood can be lightly planed so that the cut is placed where you intended.

Using a screw driver

A cordless screw driver is a great asset as it will drive in screws effortlessly. Drill a shallow pilot hole which is the same diameter as the straight part of the screw just beyond the head. This will make sure that the screw goes straight into the wood.

PAPIER-MACHE

This is a fascinating craft, inexpensive and versatile. Practically no equipment is needed other than a mould and one or two kitchen utensils.

You can make your own flour and water paste but it is much easier to buy a packet of wallpaper paste.

Layering method

In this, pasted strips of paper are applied to a mould and left to dry. Afterwards, the papier-mâché shell is lifted off. Inflated balloons make round or oval shapes. All sorts of other items can be used as moulds, but none of the shapes must be undercut, meaning that they must not contain

portions which jut out over other parts of the shape.

Basic technique

Grease the mould all over with petroleum jelly. Tear newspaper into small strips about ½in (12mm) wide and 2in (5cm) long. Dampen the strips in water and apply to the mould, overlapping the strips. Smooth each strip into place.

For the second and subsequent layers, put some mixed wallpaper paste into a shallow bowl and dip the paper strips into it. Apply all over the mould, then apply a third layer of pasted strips, this time working in the other direction. If the first and second layers were horizontal, make

89

this layer vertical: this helps to strengthen the structure. Add another layer of strips, working in the first direction again, and continue until the layers are thick enough to hold the shape. You may need 6-10 layers.

Technique for balloon moulds
Before applying the first layer of newspaper strips, wet the balloon thoroughly and prop it up in a small bowl for ease of handling. Apply the first layer, allowing the moisture on the balloon to soak through the strips so

making them adhere to its surface. By making the first layer adhere to the balloon in this way it will be easy to remove it when the papier-mâché is dry. Continue to cover the balloon as above.

Drying
Papier-mâché will take several days to dry completely. Keep the mould propped up and allow it to dry naturally in a warm, dry place. When drying the balloon mould you may arrange it with the tied neck upright on a flat surface. In this way a flat base will form on the balloon. If you are making the egg on page 60, you will cut away the base so that you can insert the puppet.

Painting
Paint the papier-mâché with white emulsion paint, then decorate with acrylic or poster paints. Finish by painting with a coat of diluted PVA adhesive. This adhesive is used as wood glue just as it comes from the bottle.

Papier-mâché on an armature
Since the armature, as used in the model of the Tyrannosaurus rex, will not be removed from the model, the first layer may be applied using paste to make it adhere. The shape of the dinosaur will need an extra thickening in some parts of its modelling. Some areas may be padded with crumpled newspaper or even crumpled baking foil to give the correct shape. Continue to cover the crumpled padding with further layers of newsprint.

Leave the work to dry. This may be speeded by putting the model into a very low oven. Paint as for the layered method.

TOYMAKING

Stitching
A sewing machine is useful for toy making but not essential. Machine sewing saves time and looks neat, but hand sewing can be just as strong and hard wearing. Felt toys are best sewn by hand. Oversew the pieces together on the wrong side within ⅛in (3mm) of the edge, taking about 12 stitches to 1in (2.5cm).

Scissors
You will need at least three pairs of scissors. Dressmaking scissors with sharp blades and pointed tips are needed for cutting out fabrics. A small pair of pointed embroidery scissors is useful for trimming seams, snipping into seam allowances and cutting threads. Lastly, find an old pair of scissors

and keep them for cutting out cardboard and paper.

Pins and needles

Choose glass-headed dressmaking pins because these are easy to see, and there is less likelihood of their becoming misplaced or left inside a toy. The size of needle is a matter of personal preference, but medium-sized crewel needles, which have long eyes and are easy to thread, are best for general sewing, while fine needles are best for hand sewing felt toys.

Stuffing tools

While sewing a toy you should try to calculate the areas which will be most complicated to stuff and leave extra openings in the seams so that these areas may be easily stuffed. Blunt pencils or large knitting needles make useful stuffing tools. Pointed tweezers may be useful when stuffing tiny pieces such as the arms and legs of the Corythosaurus family.

Stuffing the toy

Polyester washable toy filling is ideal for stuffing as it is light and easy to handle. Kapok makes good stuffing too, but you cannot wash toys stuffed with it as it will stain the fabric used to make the toy. When filling a toy, put the stuffing into any complicated part a very little at a time. The main portions can be filled using larger pieces of stuffing.

Closing the openings

When the toy is finished, close openings left for stuffing with tiny oversewing stitches, pushing any seam allowances to the inside as you work.

APPLIQUE WITH FUSIBLE INTERFACING

Fusible interfacing is a very useful material for appliqué. First, it can be used to fuse the raw edges of fabric so that is does not fray or ravel. Second, it can be used to bond the top fabric into position on the background fabric so that there is no need to stitch it in place.

Draw or trace the appliqué shape on to the paper side of the fusible interfacing. Remember to reverse the motif if it is not symmetrical. Cut roughly around the motif, leaving about ½in (12mm) margin.

Spread the appliqué fabric right side down on the ironing board. Set the iron to the temperature appropriate to the fabric. Lay the fusible interfacing shape, web side down, on the fabric. Press with the hot iron to fuse it to the fabric. Lower the iron straight on to the interfacing shape, leave it in position for a few seconds, then lift straight off. Do not iron to and fro across the fabric or you may distort the shape of the motif. If the motif does not appear to have fused at the first attempt, repeat the process until it has done so.

Cut out round the line marked on the paper backing. Peel off the backing paper. Lay the motif, face up on the background fabric.

Using the iron setting that is appropriate to both fabrics, fuse the motif to the background, again using the press and lift method outlined above.

FABRIC PAINTING

Fabric painting is great fun. Once you have invested in a few fabric pens you will be able to decorate many garments with them.

Choose white or light coloured fabrics to decorate. Practise the technique first on a spare piece of fabric. Wash, rinse and dry the article, then iron it perfectly flat.

Trace the design on to a large piece of white paper and draw over the lines firmly with a black felt-tipped pen, then position it under the garment and pin it securely in place.

You should be able to see the black outlines though the fabric. Spread the garment on a flat surface, then draw the motif with the fabric crayons or paints. Remember to fill in large areas with evenly applied strokes.

Fix the design by covering it with a clean cloth and ironing it for one to two minutes with the iron on the hottest setting.

If you want to emphasize your design with puff paint, hold the capped bottle upside down and shake it well.

Again, it is a good idea to practise first on a spare piece of fabric. You must have a backing paper underneath your work to prevent the paint seeping through to other areas.

Remove the bottle cap and hold the bottle so that its nozzle is just above the fabric. Squeeze gently so that a consistent stream of paint emerges.

Give the bottle a shake downwards from time to time to remove any air bubbles. If the nozzle becomes blocked you may free it with a pin.

Let the paint dry overnight. To puff it, turn the fabric so that the back is facing you, and iron it very lightly for one minute with the iron on a hot setting.

Do not wash the garment until the paint has been fixed for three days, then hand wash carefully without rubbing. Iron on the back of the garment, to avoid lifting the puffy paint.

PAINTING WOOD

Wood should be very smooth before painting and this may take several sandings, finishing with the very finest grade. Nails should be punched below the surface and any holes or blemishes filled with wood filler.

An extra fine finish can be given to wood if, when you have finished the final sanding, the work is wetted with clean water. Leave it to dry and the grain will have raised. A final sanding with a fine grade paper will give a silky smoothness, ideal for painting or varnishing.

If you are making a toy, take great care that only non-toxic paint is used. Always take the advice of the supplier. Tiny tins of gloss or matt craft paints, available in a wide range of colours, are ideal for painting small toys. There is also a kind of craft paint that is diluted with water. This type of paint is used when you want the wood grain to show.

Getting a good finish

Getting a really good painted finish takes time and preparation. Prime the wood with primer, then apply two thin coats of a suitable undercoat. Diluted emulsion paint makes a good undercoat. Rub the dry undercoat smooth again if bits of paint have stuck to the surface.

Before applying the final gloss coat, choose a fairly warm day if possible and do not wear anything woolly! Close the windows if there is a breeze which might bring hairs and dust into contact with your work.

Dip the bristles of the brush into the paint and draw the brush against the side of the tin to remove excess paint and any drips. Apply the paint lightly and immediately begin to brush out. This means spreading the paint in all directions from where you applied it. You will be surprised how far one brush-load of paint will go! Try to achieve a really thin coat of paint over the surface. Finally, brush out with all the strokes going in one direction lifting the brush into the air at the end of a stroke. In a few minutes, the surface will have smoothed itself out. Leave to dry, under cover if possible.

SALT DOUGH

A model should be left to go cold before painting. Poster paints come in bright colours and are easy to use. They are also non-toxic, so are suitable for children to use. All you do is put a ¼-teaspoon of paint in a painter's palette and gradually add small amounts of water until you get the consistency you like. If you add too much water, the paint will not be bright, so add more paint.

Two sizes of paint brush are useful: an average size (no. 5) and a thin brush (no. 0). Use the soft-bristle variety.

Varnishing

Use clear varnish, the thicker the better. To test for the thickest one, just shake the cans. Use a painter's brush to apply the varnish, and make sure that all sides are varnished. If you use a thin, watery varnish, apply several coats. Always varnish the back and front of a model as it helps to keep moisture out.

Trouble-shooting
There are various ways of saving a model that seems to be going wrong.

Blistering (air bubbles)
This means that the oven is too hot. First reduce the temperature. Using a water spray, wet the bubble and prick it. Then gently press out the air using your fingers and smooth over the surface. If the surface dough is too hard to do this, break the blister and fill it with fresh dough.

Parts fall off
Insufficient water has been used when sticking the parts together. Either use some fresh dough to bind the two sections together, or use a glue (wood glue or a similar type).

Cracking and splitting
This tends to happen across large, flattish areas, probably because the dough is too wet. Dough expands while baking and contracts again while cooling, causing the dough to split. If you reduce the proportion of water in the mixture, this will mean less expansion and therefore less contraction.

Another method of preventing cracking is to slow down the cooling down process. Either turn off the oven once the figures are rock hard and leave them in it to cool down gradually, or, if you have to take them out, wrap them in a towel and leave them in a warmish place.

Caring for salt-dough figures
Salt dough is made from organic products and needs to be preserved and cared for. If you do this, your models will last forever. They should be kept dry and free from moisture at all times. Check that they are not left on a window ledge, where condensation may occur, near damp walls, or out of doors. If they get wet, the dough will become soggy and expand, eventually splitting and rotting.

REMOVING ADHESIVES
If you are doing craftwork, inevitably you will be using glues and adhesives of different kinds. And, almost as inevitably, some adhesives will get onto clothes or furnishings. Adhesive manufacturers are very good about helping with advice about solvents for their products. Some will even supply solvents direct if you write to them. In general, the first step in glue first aid is to scrape off any deposit and then proceed as follows:

Clear adhesive
On the skin, wash first, then remove any residue with nail varnish remover. On clothing and furnishings, hold a pad of absorbent rag on the underside, dab with non-oily nail varnish remover on the right side.

Epoxy adhesive
Lighter fuel or cellulose thinners will remove adhesive from the hands. On fabrics, hold a rag pad under the glue stain, dab with cellulose thinners on the right side. On synthetic fibres, use lighter fuel.

Adhesive tape residue
White spirit or cellulose thinners may do it. Or try nail varnish remover. Adhesives vary and you will have to experiment.

Latex adhesive
Lift off as much as possible before the adhesive hardens. Keep the glue soft with cold water and rub with a cloth. Treat any stains with liquid dry cleaner. Scrape off any deposits with a pencil rubber.

Dinosaurs in this book

Anatosaurus
(A-*nat-o*-saw-rus)
The front of this plant-eating dinosaur's head was bill-shaped. It had large fleshy nostrils on either side of its face. 40ft (12.2m) long.

Ankylosaurus
(Ank-il-o-*saw*-rus)
An armoured dinosaur that walked on all four feet. At the end of its tail was a large lump of bone with spikes, which was used as a club. 15ft (4.75m) long.

Archaeopteryx
(Ark-ee-*op*-ter-ix)
One of the first birds. It had feathers, also teeth in its beak and claws on the front of its wings. 1ft (30cm) wing span.

Brachiosaurus
(Brack-ee-o-*saw*-rus)
This was the biggest known land animal ever. It was plant eating and its front legs were longer than its hind legs so that it craned its neck like a giraffe. 35ft (11m) tall.

Centrosaurus
(Sen-tro-*saw*-rus)
This dinosaur was similar to Triceratops with a bony frill at the back of its head, but it only had one long horn which was on the front of its head. 30ft (9.1m) long.

Corythosaurus
(Kor-ith-o-*saw*-rus)
A plant-eating dinosaur that walked mainly on its hind legs. It had a big bony crest on its head and it could swim well. 30ft (9.1m) long.

Deinonychus
(Die-non-*nike*-us)
A small, fierce, meat-eating dinosaur. 9ft (2.8m) long.

Dimetrodon
(Di-*meet*-ro-don)
This early meat-eating ancestor of the mammals had a huge "sail" on its back. 9ft (2.8m) long.

Dimorphodon
(Die-*morf*-o-don)
An early flying reptile with teeth and a long tail. 4ft (1.2m) wing span.

Diplodocus
(Dip-lo-*dock*-us)
A plant-eating dinosaur which walked on all four feet. It often waded into water. 90ft (27.5m) long.

Pachycephalosaurus
(Pack-ee-*seff*-alo-saws-rus)
This plant-eating dinosaur walked on its hind legs. Its domed head was made of thick bone. It may have fought using this as a battering ram. 14ft (4.3m) long.

Rhamphorhyncus
(Ram-fo-*rink*-us)
Another of the early flying reptiles which did not have feathers and lived on fish. 3ft (96cm) wing span.

Stegosaurus
(Steg-o-*saw*-rus)
An armoured dinosaur which walked on all four feet. It had two rows of big bony plates on its back with two pairs of long sharp spikes on its tail. Its small head had a brain the size of a walnut. 20ft (6.1m) long.

Triceratops
(Tri-*sera*-tops)
This plant-eating dinosaur was a savage fighter. It had two large horns at the back of its head and a smaller one on its beak-like nose. 30ft (9.1m) long.

Tryannosaurus
(Ty-*ran*-o-saw-rus)
This was the largest flesh eating animal that ever existed. The head alone was over 4ft (1.23m) long while the teeth were 6in (5cm) long. The tiny front legs, with two fingered hands, must have been almost useless. 16ft (5m) tall, 40ft (12m) long.

Velociraptor
(Ve-*loss*-ee-raptor)
A small, fierce, meat-eating dinosaur which hunted for food in packs. 9ft (2.7m) long.

ACKNOWLEDGEMENT
The author thanks Dr Richard PS Jefferies
of the British Museum of Natural History
for technical help and advice

96